IT MAKES ZERO SENSE

PATRICK SAMAHA

IT MAKES ZERO SENSE

Embracing Life's Nonsense

PATRICK SAMAHA

It Makes Zero Sense
Copyright © 2024 Patrick Samaha
First published in 2024

Print: 978-1-76124-202-1
E-book: 978-1-76124-203-8
Hardback: 978-1-76124-204-5

All rights reserved. No part of this book may be reproduced, stored in a retrieval system, or transmitted by any means (electronic, mechanical, photocopying, recording, or otherwise) without written permission from the author.

Because of the dynamic nature of the Internet, any web addresses or links contained in this book may have changed since publication and may no longer be valid. The information in this book is based on the author's experiences and opinions. The views expressed in this book are solely those of the author and do not necessarily reflect the views of the publisher; the publisher hereby disclaims any responsibility for them.

The author of this book does not dispense any form of medical, legal, financial, or technical advice either directly or indirectly. The intent of the author is solely to provide information of a general nature to help you in your quest for personal development and growth. In the event you use any of the information in this book, the author and the publisher assume no responsibility for your actions. If any form of expert assistance is required, the services of a competent professional should be sought.

Publishing information
Publishing and design facilitated by Passionpreneur Publishing
A division of Passionpreneur Organization Pty Ltd
ABN: 48640637529

Melbourne, VIC | Australia
www.passionpreneurpublishing.com

To all those who dare to embrace the perplexing journey of untangling negativity, resisting change, transforming confusion into clarity, and discovering the profound beauty that lies within the paradox of 'zero sense'.

This book is dedicated to those who embrace the paradoxical world of "zero", where nothingness gives birth to boundless creativity, where negatives become positives, and where the power of the void illuminates the path to limitless possibilities. May you find inspiration in chaos, wisdom in absurdity, and beauty in the enigmatic dance of zero as you embark on this journey through the realms of imagination.

This dedication can apply to anyone who resonates with the theme of my book, which explores the concept of "zero" and its nature in various contexts. They might be wonderers in life and the workplace, or people who want a fresh start in their life or career.

TABLE OF CONTENTS

Acknowledgments ix
Preface: "It Makes Zero Sense." xi

Chapter 0	Zero	1
Chapter 1	The Zero Picture	21
Chapter 2	Unlearn	35
Chapter 3	The Nature of Number Zero	47
Chapter 4	Mathematical Mysteries	59
Chapter 5	If All Knowledge is Available	73
Chapter 6	Media Rarities and Real-Life Impacts	85
Chapter 6.5	Puzzlers	99
Chapter 7	No Offense	107
Chapter 8	Pineapple on Pizza (Things That Don't Make Sense)	115
Chapter 9	The Art of Nothing	127
Chapter 10	Acceptance	135

Author Bio 145
Extras 149

ACKNOWLEDGMENTS

I'D LIKE TO thank everyone who is part of my life, particularly my family and friends. I thank people who will come into my life in the future, and equally those who aren't in my life anymore; without them, life became more meaningful and magical.

Many people in my life have helped to make me the way I am whether by showing me who to be or who not to be. First is my family, who have always been with me throughout my life.

My mother Hilda dedicated all her life to my success and consciousness. My twin brother and best friend Dany has basically lived every breath with me and supported me for fifty-odd years.

My wife Salma, for being who she is and holding the fort through thick and thin; my three beautiful girls Ayla, Sima, and Raya, who gave the world a new meaning with their existence; and my mother-in-law, for all her love and support.

I thank my close friends and family who always believed in me: Special thanks to my new great friends, for their friendship and trust, to Dr. Fouad Alame whose support and friendship is a great gift, and to many more who, with patience and an open heart, lent me their ear during the journey of crafting this book. Your attentive listening, insightful feedback, and unwavering support have been invaluable. May you find inspiration in the exploration of "zero" and its transformative power, just as you have enriched my own understanding with your presence.

I would like to give a big thank you to people who hate me, as I have learned to believe that haters are in fact secret admirers.

Thank you to my partners and supporters. In this book, I specifically want to thank some hidden talent who, I am confident, will rise and become great individuals: Pia, for all her coordination and support; and Tasmiyah, who helped me organize across all this journey. Special thanks to Vidhan, who is the most loyal person I've worked with; and my publisher Passionpreneur (Moustafa and his team), who gave me confidence across this amazing journey. They all make zero sense to me 😊.

PREFACE
"IT MAKES ZERO SENSE."
THE HIGHS OF NUMBER ZERO

LIKE ME, I'M sure you have heard the statement, "It makes zero sense." You might even have said it a few times. It's said when we just don't get what someone is saying, or you can't see the logic, right? I was in the same boat as you: Zero was always a nothing, or a negative reference. Then I started to think about it more, not the statement but the number zero. What if we removed the negative connotation and thought of zero as a starting point? I started to think more about what zero could represent if it were perceived as more than just a number.

What I discovered was infinite possibility. Yes, zero drove me to think of infinity. It's fascinating how these complete opposites can be equally strong and full of hope and change. What you will see in this book is a call to adopt a zero mindset, one that will open a new era in how we see things, and more importantly how we act upon them. In a world obsessed with adding value, multiplying outcomes, and elevating numbers, there stands a silent hero: the number ZERO.

It makes zero sense. Let me elaborate.

Zero is not just the absence of value, but a powerful trigger in the art of elimination, primarily when it comes to refusing the negatives. Starting from zero, or *restarting* from zero, is challenging yet powerful. Much more complicated than you think, it allows you to do better. It will enable you to reset your efforts and begin anew, often with a clearer perspective or renewed determination.

Let's take the analogy of running a race with a timer.

When you start a running race of, say, 200 meters, you press the timer button on your watch and start running. When you reach the end of the 200 meters, you have achieved a specific time, say 2 minutes. Then you do it again and get 1 minute and 50 seconds. The next day you do the same thing, always starting from zero and trying to achieve better results. Then it hits you: The closer you are to zero, the faster you are. This becomes your motivation to wake up and do it again.

Each time you begin anew, you can improve upon your previous performance. Starting from zero symbolizes a fresh start, free of past limitations or setbacks. It encourages a mindset of continuous improvement and growth.

Like the act of timing yourself, each attempt presents an opportunity to learn, adapt, and push yourself further. The progress made from each iteration reflects physical improvement, mental resilience, and discipline. By consistently striving to better their performance, individuals can gradually inch closer to their goals and achieve tremendous success.

Moreover, the notion of starting from zero emphasizes the importance of persistence. Regardless of past achievements or failures, each new beginning offers the chance to strive for excellence and surpass previous limits. Starting from zero fosters a mindset of progress, innovation, and continual self-improvement. It encourages you to embrace challenges, learn from experiences, and relentlessly pursue your aspirations. As you saw in this simple example, the closer someone is to zero, the more vividly they're showing both the speed and the intensity of commitment and dedication.

Now, let's take that analogy and make it into a theory. We can start thinking of other things we do and how getting closer to zero helps us win. In such an exercise, zero becomes the value, not the absence of value. It becomes a powerful way to be greater than before. As we'll explore in the coming chapters, the concept of zero has its roots in ancient civilizations, from the Sumerians to the Mayans, and has been an instrumental figure in mathematical, philosophical, and existential discussions across millennia.

But zero's true power lies beyond the domain of a mere digit. Zero represents a balance, a neutral point, and in many ways, a fresh start. Take daily life as an example. Every time I take my kids out as a family, we start in an anger mode (call it an Arab hot-blooded style), but after the peaks of this attitude, we all calm down, actually having fun when we reach zero noise.

"Elimination of negatives" might sound like an act of reduction. Yet in the grander scheme of things, it's a process of purification, simplification, and getting to the heart of what truly matters. By subtracting the unnecessary, we often add value.

In the chapters ahead, we'll delve into the essence of zero, exploring its many faces, including "zeroing out", which can be applied to declutter our minds, refine our focus in business and, more importantly, enhance our personal lives while reshaping our thinking.

Come with me on this journey into nothingness, where we'll discover that, sometimes, we must first embrace the power of zero to reach the peak of our potential.

Let's go from "it makes zero sense" to making zero the starting point for everything.

Patrick Samaha

0

ZERO

A STARTING POINT

IT IS FASCINATING how aging, or maybe we should call it growing, rewires your mind. We go from only seeing potential in our lives to focusing on efficiency and perfection. I used to believe that what people didn't know, they couldn't understand. How can you identify something that you never think of? If it is not in your mind, it cannot be in your life; you cannot talk about it.

Let's take a magician as an example. When they perform a trick, you are confused: What you can't see, you can't believe, right? The secret is only visible to the artist or the maker themselves. They know how the story ends, but you are waiting to see the outcome, which gives the magician power over you.

Is the magician deceiving you or creating a lie? We have an Arabic saying (حبل الأكاذيب قصير) that means "The rope of lies is short"; eventually, people will find out, like at the end of a magic trick. Similarly, we live in a world where everyone is making up a story instead of living one, leading false or fake lives. Realizing this allowed me to lean towards the life I could talk about instead of living. Do you feel the same way? Think of social media: You see great pictures and stories from the outside, but how true are they?

I remember my twenties. Like my friends, I found it difficult to navigate the uncertainties and aspirations of early adulthood. The feeling of being at the beginning of one's adult life, full of ambition and potential, is indeed a unique and robust experience. I grew up in an environment where success and stability seemed elusive, presenting significant challenges. The lack of hope or clear paths to success can be disheartening and overwhelming. Yet, individuals often discover their resilience and determination during these times of struggle and uncertainty.

The prospect of studying in college and embarking on a journey to define one's future can be both exciting and daunting. The endless possibilities ahead and the mystery of who you will become can be a source of motivation. Embracing the unknown can fuel a drive to explore, learn and grow, propelling you to pursue your dreams and aspirations.

While the path may be uncertain and the challenges tough, my willingness to confront these obstacles head-on gave me strength and courage. Facing adversity and overcoming personal struggles often make individuals more potent, more resilient, and better-equipped to navigate the complexities of life.

Remember, the journey of self-discovery and personal growth is ongoing. Embrace the challenges, cherish the victories, and stay true to your aspirations. Your experiences, triumphs, and trials will shape the person you become and the path you ultimately carve for yourself.

I remember my first job interview. During the last semester of my bachelor's degree, I landed an interview with an automotive company. My strategy was to present myself as someone I wanted to be rather than the person I was, so I borrowed a fancy suit and watch and went for the job. When I reached the location and found myself among people the same age as me, I felt very proud of my choice: I looked like the interviewer rather than the interviewee! This gave me confidence and allowed me to stand out from the others. My appearance made me feel entitled to the job.

Once I got the job, I realized that if I could hold onto this new image long enough, I would eventually change and feel fuller in my life. But inauthenticity, or at least attempting to play a role for external satisfaction, often becomes an addiction. When you start being accepted, you want more. In the late 90s, I changed countries for my career. If getting that first job was difficult, leaving everyone I knew to start afresh with complete strangers was much harder.

This is where zero becomes a solution or an answer, rather than an emptiness.

When I look at my personal journey in life, I think of how, when I was younger, I had zero chances. Maybe it was because of the place I grew up, Lebanon, an environment of civil war. It was a country that offered me the basics, but I had no one to look up to from a career perspective, including my relatives and my circle of friends. I never knew who the person in me was, and never, in my mind, could I conceive of the person I would become.

I had two options in my life: to act or to wait. I decided to act, and action became my biggest tool to achieve goals or learn lessons. I am not yet talking about achieving success. It was the desire to act, instead of waiting, that drove me to become better than before. My first motivation was thinking that action would take me somewhere better than yesterday, which was my first big win! And when I look back, I see this was my starting point. I had always felt bad about where I was from, who I was, until it hit me: Zero chances in life allow you to have hero possibilities.

I formed the belief that when it seems impossible for you to achieve something, you become the definition of possible when you *do* achieve it. Even brands have used this in their slogans: "Impossible is nothing"—Adidas!

Over time, I've learned about success and error. Success comes to you in three main ways: through hard work, through luck, and through carrying yourself forward. Maintaining success always demands hard work and a bit of luck, so how do you ensure you minimize risk? For starters, eliminate the negatives, ensure zero issues, and reduce the chances of being unlucky.

Embarking on the journey toward success is like setting sail on an uncharted sea, where the winds of fortune and the currents of effort intermingle in a complex dance. As we navigate these waters, we understand that success is not merely a destination but a dynamic process shaped by our actions and circumstances, in conjunction with various other factors. Through contemplation and experience, we gather insights into the delicate balance between effort and chance, learning how to harness both to chart our course toward prosperity.

The Virtue of Diligence

One theme resonates with unwavering clarity in human achievement: the irreplaceable role of hard work in the pursuit of success. From laborers struggling in the fields to visionaries striving to revolutionize industries, history is crowded with examples of individuals who have propelled themselves to greatness through perseverance and determination. Indeed, hard work is the bedrock upon which the structure of success is built, providing the scaffolding necessary to elevate dreams into reality.

But what defines hard work? Is it simply the exertion of physical effort, or does it encompass a broader spectrum of endeavors? To crack this enigma, we need to delve into the essence of diligence: the unchangeable commitment to one's goals, the stubbornness to overcome obstacles, and the relentless pursuit of excellence. Through discipline and dedication, we transform fleeting aspirations into enduring achievements, laying the groundwork for success to take root and flourish.

It is crucial to carry yourself forward, pushing yourself daily until it becomes an addiction, or else you won't be successful. You will fail many times, but when you learn how to fail less, you start to win more; with time, you will see yourself as a winner, and you can mark minor points of success that drive you forward. Anything can be recorded as a win, as "better than yesterday", so whatever you want your journey to be, wait for your wins, and you shall win more.

Work is never easy; it requires you to believe in something for the future, a goal for yourself that you can achieve in less than twenty years. Start with goals for a week or a month and see how long it takes to reach them, then start adding *more* goals. This requires effort on your side. Work harder until you see yourself working smarter; anything you put in will get you to your goals faster. Then, small goals become more prominent, and achieving bigger ones will get you on the road to success.

The Unstable Finger of Fortune

As we navigate the twisted corridors of fate, we encounter an unstable companion, "the hand of luck", whose whims shape the contours of our journey. Luck, that elusive mistress, holds sway over the outcomes of our endeavors, bestowing favor upon some while casting others adrift on the sea of uncertainty. Yet, to attribute success solely to luck is to oversimplify the intricate tapestry of human experience.

Luck is a multifaceted phenomenon. It is woven from the threads of opportunity, timing, and chance encounters. It manifests in unexpected windfalls and fortuitous circumstances, altering the course of our lives in ways both profound and unforeseen. Yet luck is not merely a passive force but also a dynamic one, responsive to the currents of our efforts and intentions.

In the dance between hard work and luck, we find a delicate equilibrium. It is a symbiotic relationship, with our actions shaping the terrain so fortune can find us. By cultivating an environment conducive to serendipity and embracing uncertainty with open arms, we invite luck to guide us toward our aspirations, transforming happenstance into opportunity and chance into destiny.

If you feel you are unlucky, you can change that: Adopt a mindset of change and being better, and you will see yourself getting luckier. I don't mean that by doing so, you will find miracles. Your hard work and action will get you results; you will find yourself feeling lucky. When you operate intelligently and with a purpose, the outcome of that might look lucky to the outside world, but you will realize that it comes from what you have put into it.

As we conclude our exploration of hard work, luck, and the continuation of past successes, we are reminded of the complicated threads that bind these elements together. Success is a collaborative endeavor, a symphony of effort, opportunity, and persistence. In the symphony of life, each note contributes to the melody, each chord resonates with purpose, and each crescendo heralds the promise of a brighter tomorrow.

As we set sail into the unknown, let us remember the lessons from our journey. The secret to unlocking the boundless potential resides within us all, the possibility to chart our own course, shape our destiny, and discover the true meaning of success.

Let's see how zero uncovers possibilities instead of nothingness!

Did you ever hear of the "Tenth Man" theory? It is used in decision-making, and also qualifies for *non*-decision-making. The theory suggests that in a group or team making decisions, it is essential to have someone play the role of the "Tenth Man". This individual takes on the responsibility of providing a contrarian viewpoint, even if it contradicts the consensus or prevailing opinion within the group.

The rationale behind the Tenth Man theory is to guard against groupthink and ensure that all possibilities are considered before making a decision. By deliberately seeking out dissenting opinions, the group can challenge assumptions, identify blind spots, and uncover potential risks or alternative solutions that may have been overlooked.

Having a tenth person allows you to challenge the thinking, to do better and think of alternative ways to reach perfection. Imagine yourself in a meeting with ten people in the room. Say you are all planning a business, or launching a product, and together you reach a conclusion about how you will proceed. The last thing to do is nominate a tenth person to destroy that plan. This is a must. Having someone in your group whose goal is to rethink what everyone else has decided allows you to reduce error. And this makes for a better business or product. Their role is not just to say no; they need to dig deeper, find problems, and more importantly *explain* them to make sure everyone understands where they can do better.

Allow time to explore other options. Don't just agree and move to execution; instead, add another layer of thought and effort before you sign off. Keep this tenth person always alive in your life: perhaps as a way of thinking, a process of analysis that allows you to genuinely believe in your decisions. We all want what is best for us or our business , but how do we know if we've made the right decision? You can only know after you've made it. Take a business idea: You develop it, invest heavily, and wait for the results; only then can you know for sure whether it was the right one.

Early on in my life, I found myself always hiding problems, what people don't see doesn't exist, right? That's what I believed. But then I realized that this strategy can only work for attracting business, not maintaining it. Hiding is never successful; it will eventually show, just like lying. Now, I am always transparent, which maximizes the positives and eliminates the negatives.

At the beginning of my career, I could not say no to anything. Now I say no a lot more often so that I can succeed more. I didn't come to this conclusion overnight. I was always afraid of missing out: I felt that if I said no, I might lose the opportunity. But whenever I landed a deal that wasn't right, it always crumbled to dust, and the relationship with the client would also be destroyed. I started to lose credibility. So I had to learn to block the fear of missing out and embrace the *no* when I knew the deal was not sustainable. It made it harder to win, but the win was better and more durable.

I am reminded here of something Leonardo di Caprio said. As a young actor, he was always saying "I can do any scene." It resulted in him receiving fewer opportunities than he would have if he'd been honest. But when he stood tall and accepted who he was, he started to get the parts in great films that made him a credible actor.

Adopting the mindset of being true to myself allowed me to have real success. I began thinking through decisions to make sure I did not settle for my faults. I would rather go back and make things right than let a problem go unnoticed. It is harder, for sure, but it allows you to choose the sort of business you want. Having zero errors, or close to zero, is mandatory for success these days.

I think of myself as a self-made man. By that, I mean that I started on my own and became what I am from my own experiences. I'm not talking about success or money, now. When you start in life you face many barriers, and how you proceed defines who you are and the person you ought to be. I climbed the ladder of career in my own way, without ever having a mentor. Once I accepted that life experiences were my only school, I started to take them more seriously and learn from them. I packaged myself as refined, but I'll admit that I did have gaps. There is no shame in admitting this sort of thing to yourself, as you have to accept your faults before you can begin to fix them. As I evolved, I started to identify problems in a very analytical way. Let me explain. If you appreciate math like me, thinking of a problem analytically encourages you to find a solution. So don't be afraid to look for the problems within yourself or your approach. When you turn something into a challenge to solve, you will have better chances of fixing it.

Imagine you feel low this week but don't understand why. Write down what happened the week before. Look at it analytically. Once you have mapped out the entire period and looked at all possible scenarios, you will start to see where the issue was. That's the necessary step to solving it.

My learning in life progressed by seeking problems to solve. It's a little like a game. I use it to train my mind. Seeking problems and solving them has enabled me to fill the gaps in my understanding. Slowly, I could see the problems decrease and solutions alone become the main driver of my approach.

This was my personal story of success from nothing. Looking for problems one at a time, and fixing them one at a time, led me to a zero-problem mindset. I am reminded of this by many small moments in my career that shaped me to be better in some way, moments including never quitting on a project until it was completed. Although I am mostly motivated by competition, when there is none, I compete with my own past.

Today I am working with a zero mindset to run a successful company to eliminate negatives, draft a book, and change the world. A bit too optimistic, perhaps? I believe that if you aim high, your standards will follow and reach higher, too. The funny thing about this is, it's always easier to grow, but it's harder to fix issues. Growth towards achievement is infinitely possible, but reaching zero in negatives will always be aspirational. That is, it is not possible to achieve in reality. For example, you can aspire to make more money, but you can never aspire to make it in a perfect manner. I am a living example, one of many, of a zero-negativity mindset. It's what you need to keep on your toes to achieve greatness.

Success is Based on Zero Errors

Let me give you an example of that statement "Success is based on zero errors" by looking at Formula 1, a highly technical numbers- and data-driven sport. Formula 1 is highly competitive. There are ten teams, with every team having two drivers (a lead driver and a second driver). Some think that it is all about winning races, but trust me, it's far more complicated than that. What happens within an F1 team is a magic of strategies to create champions.

Hundreds of team members work efficiently to overcome obstacles in every lap of every qualifier or race. Data is king. Teams rely on a vast array of sensors and real-time data analytics to make split-second decisions that can mean the difference between victory and defeat. An example of how one data error can lose a race can be illustrated through a hypothetical scenario involving fuel calculations.

The Scenario: The Fuel Calculation Error

Imagine the team of a leading driver, let's call him Michael, in the final laps of the Monaco Grand Prix. The team's data analysts have been working tirelessly, calculating and recalculating the optimal fuel load to make sure Michael can push hard to the finish without carrying unnecessary weight.

The Error

Due to a minor software glitch in the team's data analysis tools, the fuel consumption rate for Michael's car is miscalculated by a mere 0.5%. This seems insignificant, but in the high-stakes world of F1, it's a colossal error. The team mistakenly informs Michael that he has enough fuel to finish the race at maximum power.

The Consequence

Encouraged by his team, Michael pushes his car to the limit, eating up the track and widening his lead. However, as he enters the final lap, the unthinkable happens: His car starts to sputter and lose power. The data error meant the team underestimated the fuel required to finish the race. Michael watches helplessly as one, two, three competitors overtake him in the final moments, relegating him from a certain victory to a heartbreaking fourth place.

The Lesson

This scenario highlights not just the importance of accurate data, but also how even the smallest error in data analysis can have monumental consequences. Every bit of information, from tire pressure to fuel load, must be precisely calculated to ensure a car can perform at its peak from start to finish. In a sport where races can be won or lost by fractions of a second, there's no room for error.

Unlocking the Power of Zero

From Eliminating Negatives to Achieving Balance, and Cultivating a Legacy of Success

I decided to write my book to help intrapreneurs[1] and corporates struggling with stalled growth, unmet objectives, and poor company culture. I wanted to introduce them to the power of the zero mindset, a way of thinking that eliminates negatives and achieves balance. Using it can create a positive legacy that betters you own business and adds value to others. In life, whether personal or professional, we always need to reduce our errors to be the best version of ourselves and have a better chance of succeeding. This is both a journey and an adoption of a mindset to succeed.

---

1 Employees with an entrepreneurial mindset.

It is not about trying to achieve a state without problems or challenges; rather, it's about resetting our approach to both perceiving issues and tackling them. It's a methodology that encourages stripping away clutter, negative thoughts, inefficient processes, and unproductive habits to focus on core values and strengths. This mindset prioritizes clarity, simplicity, and purpose, enabling a more focused and effective strategy towards personal and professional goals.

Why Develop the Zero Mindset?

In a complex world in constant change, the zero mindset serves as a beacon of simplicity and effectiveness. For businesses, it means adopting leaner processes, fostering a culture of continuous improvement, and enhancing agility. For individuals, it means minimizing distractions and negative influences, focusing on growth and learning, and cultivating resilience. This mindset is crucial for anyone looking to navigate the modern landscape of challenges with grace and efficiency, ultimately leading to more meaningful success and fulfillment.

This will lead you to becoming better, to being proud of what you can do and what you have accomplished. In a way it is a means to an end, but really it is a way of life and thought. There are no certainties to success when you are on the wrong path, only more struggles. Acting to change will help you enable your "game-on attitude" and be proud of what you will achieve. We will uncover together the power of zero, turning your obstacles to successes and finding the path that will help you reach your goals and those of the people or companies depending on you.

The Difference It Will Make

Embracing the zero mindset can profoundly impact both your life and your business. For organizations, it leads to a more engaged and productive workforce, streamlined operations, and a stronger competitive edge. Culturally, it fosters an environment of accountability, innovation, and continuous learning, laying the groundwork for a legacy of positive impact.

On a personal level, the zero mindset empowers you to become the best version of yourself. It encourages you to shed limiting beliefs, embrace failure as a stepping stone to growth, and continuously refine your approach to challenges. By focusing on what truly matters, you unlock a higher potential for success and satisfaction in your endeavors.

Throughout this book, we will explore the nuances of the zero mindset and how to implement it effectively. Don't be afraid to unlearn old habits; you need to clear yourself of fault as fast as possible. They say fail forward, learn faster to fix your mistakes so you become better and grow to meet your potential. Embrace that philosophy and the journey will equip you with tools to transform obstacles into stepping stones. Together, we will discover how the power of zero can illuminate your path, helping you achieve your goals, and make a lasting difference in the lives of those around you and the organizations you serve.

■ ■ ■

Countdown to Your Zero Mindset

1. **Shifting perspectives**: Maturity prompts in us a shift from seeing the potential to valuing efficiency and perfection, highlighting the importance of self-awareness and adaptation.

2. **Magicians' power**: Magicians control their audience by knowing the outcome of their tricks. This parallels how perception shapes reality in life.

3. **Authenticity vs. image**: Living authentically, versus crafting a persona for external validation, is a common struggle, particularly in the era of social media, where appearances can be misleading.

4. **Welcoming uncertainty**: Early adulthood is marked by uncertainty, but it's also a time for self-discovery, resilience, and determination in navigating life's complexities.

5. **Appearance and confidence**: Presenting oneself confidently, even if it means overdressing on occasion, can boost confidence and perception in professional settings.

6. **Action over waiting**: Taking action, even in the face of adversity, is critical to individual growth and success. It transforms perceived boundaries into opportunities.

7. **Balancing hard work and luck**: Success is a combination of hard work, opportunity, and luck, with perseverance being the foundation upon which achievements are built.

8. **The Tenth Man theory**: Having a contrarian perspective or considering dissenting opinions is crucial in decision-making, to avoid groupthink and ensure thorough analysis.

9. **Embracing transparency**: Transparency fosters growth and credibility, allowing individuals and businesses to address problems effectively and pursue authentic success.

10. **The power of zero**: Adopting a "zero mindset" involves eliminating negatives, embracing continuous improvement, and focusing on core values to achieve balance and meaningful success in both personal and professional life.

1

THE ZERO PICTURE

When you have zero chances, you have hero possibilities.

I LIKE THIS quote; think of it simply: Adversity can often be a catalyst for extraordinary achievements. When faced with seemingly impossible odds, people may tap into their inner resilience, creativity, and determination to overcome challenges and achieve greatness.

While some people attain fame and recognition for their accomplishments, most successful people do it quietly. There are a variety of human experiences and many paths to success.

Several factors contribute to success.

1. **Resilience**: Many successful people persevere in adversity, refusing to be deterred by setbacks or obstacles. Their resilience allows them to weather challenges and progress toward their goals.

2. **Innovation**: Some succeed by thinking outside the box and innovating in their respective fields. They may introduce new ideas, methods, or products that disrupt existing norms and carve out a niche for themselves.

3. **Impact**: Rather than seeking recognition, many successful individuals prioritize making a meaningful impact in their communities or industries. Their focus on serving others and effecting positive change drives their success, even if it goes unnoticed by the broader public.

4. **Hush-hush**: Success doesn't always come with publicity or awards. Many individuals quietly dedicate themselves to their work, consistently striving for excellence without seeking external validation.

5. **Timing**: Sometimes success results from being in the right place at the right time or seizing opportunities others have overlooked. Luck, timing, and circumstance can all affect a person's journey to success.

6. **Fulfillment**: Ultimately, success is subjective and deeply personal. Fulfillment comes from achieving goals and living according to your values, regardless of whether accomplishments make you famous.

Although the formula for success may vary from person to person, there is a common thread among successful individuals, and it is a combination of passion, perseverance, and purpose. Whether they achieve fame and recognition or quietly make their mark behind the scenes, their stories testify to the power of human resilience and the limitless potential within each of us.

That moment when you awaken to your potential for success evokes a very powerful mindset, one that allows you to give everything to win. Many of us have been in a place where giving up seems to be the only option. Well, what if we don't give up but re-engage for one last time? Wouldn't you want to give it your all the *last* time? I feel that determines a winning mindset. I want to emphasize the word "determination". When someone's life is full of weak possibilities but their determination to achieve is high, success creates a mindset to overachieve! It is quite a task to achieve something when you are struggling against the odds, but it is equally inspiring to start seeing some form of success, to see one win at a time. These can start building up to a mega-success and you become a champion.

In this chapter, we will adopt a new way to look at zero. It is usually stereotyped as negative. Zero is not bad, and it should not be defined as unsuccessful, when you place it in the right context. I believe zero is the most powerful number, and this is because it is an impossible goal to achieve. Once you learn how to overcome the errors, zero appears more as a positive result, or at least the thing that drives a positive result. Mathematically speaking, you can look at zero as nothing or as a balance. But once you see it as an achievement, it will become a practice within yourself, one that will get you to operate smarter and with more confidence.

Is Achieving Zero a Positive or Negative Myth?

My aim in this book is to expose zero and give it the credit it deserves. For starters, as a stand-alone digit, zero is insignificant; when there's a zero on the left side of a digit, it does not change anything, but put a zero on the *right* side and you see possibilities, chances, success. So, it is important. Zero is a substantial number not to be taken for granted. I could list hundreds of phrases including zero that will allow you to be better: "zero error" or "zero shortcuts" or "zero barriers" …

Let's dig into some examples from the zero zone to demonstrate this concept.

Many successful entrepreneurial ventures have emerged from initial failures. Thomas Edison famously experienced numerous setbacks before inventing the light bulb. Each "zero" moment of failure gave him valuable insights that ultimately led to his

6. **Fulfillment**: Ultimately, success is subjective and deeply personal. Fulfillment comes from achieving goals and living according to your values, regardless of whether accomplishments make you famous.

Although the formula for success may vary from person to person, there is a common thread among successful individuals, and it is a combination of passion, perseverance, and purpose. Whether they achieve fame and recognition or quietly make their mark behind the scenes, their stories testify to the power of human resilience and the limitless potential within each of us.

That moment when you awaken to your potential for success evokes a very powerful mindset, one that allows you to give everything to win. Many of us have been in a place where giving up seems to be the only option. Well, what if we don't give up but re-engage for one last time? Wouldn't you want to give it your all the *last* time? I feel that determines a winning mindset. I want to emphasize the word "determination". When someone's life is full of weak possibilities but their determination to achieve is high, success creates a mindset to overachieve! It is quite a task to achieve something when you are struggling against the odds, but it is equally inspiring to start seeing some form of success, to see one win at a time. These can start building up to a mega-success and you become a champion.

In this chapter, we will adopt a new way to look at zero. It is usually stereotyped as negative. Zero is not bad, and it should not be defined as unsuccessful, when you place it in the right context. I believe zero is the most powerful number, and this is because it is an impossible goal to achieve. Once you learn how to overcome the errors, zero appears more as a positive result, or at least the thing that drives a positive result. Mathematically speaking, you can look at zero as nothing or as a balance. But once you see it as an achievement, it will become a practice within yourself, one that will get you to operate smarter and with more confidence.

Is Achieving Zero a Positive or Negative Myth?

My aim in this book is to expose zero and give it the credit it deserves. For starters, as a stand-alone digit, zero is insignificant; when there's a zero on the left side of a digit, it does not change anything, but put a zero on the *right* side and you see possibilities, chances, success. So, it is important. Zero is a substantial number not to be taken for granted. I could list hundreds of phrases including zero that will allow you to be better: "zero error" or "zero shortcuts" or "zero barriers" …

Let's dig into some examples from the zero zone to demonstrate this concept.

Many successful entrepreneurial ventures have emerged from initial failures. Thomas Edison famously experienced numerous setbacks before inventing the light bulb. Each "zero" moment of failure gave him valuable insights that ultimately led to his success. Or let's take our personal lives. Moments of adversity or hardship can catalyze personal growth and self-discovery. A period of "zero" can be an opportunity to reflect on our values, reassess priorities, and cultivate resilience in the face of challenges. By reframing our understanding of zero and its relationship with negativity, we can embrace a more empowered mindset, one that sees challenges as opportunities and setbacks as stepping stones toward success.

It's powerful and meaningful when you place a negative concept on the right side of the zero. It's like the zero plus the negative actually make a positive, so zero is positive. But what if you place a positive idea to the right of zero? Then it becomes completely negative. So let's not think of zero as a digit; let's use it as a word and place it on the left side of a few concepts to see what we get. Consider some examples:

- **Zero doubts**: Once you are in doubt, your confidence reduces and will lead you to error and lack of motivation. To overcome self-doubt, focus on your strengths, celebrate your achievements, seek constructive feedback, and surround yourself with supportive people. Remember, everyone experiences self-doubt at times, but it's your response to it that shapes your success. Believe in yourself and your potential to achieve great things.

- **Zero integrity**: No one will be able to respect you when your integrity is questionable, and you tend to lose clients and people around you. No one will trust you or want to collaborate with you.

- **Zero barriers**: This is my favorite one. You become invincible and always want to find a solution, keep people on their feet to find a newer path, and lead them to win.

- **Zero envy**: Envy will divert your mind to hate, and you will become your own worst enemy. People will notice this and stay as far away from you as possible.

- **Zero harmony**: When people do not work together for a common purpose or goal, they tend to lose themselves. Each one will be working as an individual rather than as a team.

Zero is the absolute number when you place it on its rightful side, as perfect success is not achievable until you eliminate the minuses. So, zero before a negative is a positive and zero before a positive is a negative. Try it yourself: Add a negative statement before zero or a positive one and see what it becomes.

The concept of zero is a powerful one, often misunderstood in its importance. Yet it holds immense potential to transform our perspectives and empower us to operate at our total capacity. Rather than shying away from zero or viewing it as a void, we should embrace it.

Imagine a world where individuals are not afraid to confront their faults or acknowledge their mistakes. Instead of hiding from negativity or denying its existence, they would face it head on, using it as a springboard for personal and professional development. This shift in mindset from avoidance to acceptance opens the door to profound transformation and unlimited potential.

People cannot fathom the idea of zero. Yet, I want to change that so they can operate at maximum capacity; so they do not just rely on growth without eliminating the negatives, especially when no one else knows. In a cultural that glorifies success while disregarding failure, embracing zero becomes an act of rebellion, a declaration that our worth is not defined by our achievements but by our willingness to confront our shortcomings and strive for continuous improvement.

So let us challenge the status quo and embrace the power of zero. Let us create a world where mistakes are not viewed as weaknesses but opportunities for growth. And let's look at facts here, so the argument about zero becomes not just about a number in the numeric system but a concept upon which success balances.

Did you ever see a country with zero unemployment stats? It does not exist, as countries around the world struggle with unemployment. Some believe that others are just not trying hard, even though there is involuntary unemployment. Will we ever live in a world where everyone has a job? Impossible!

The unemployment rate in South Africa is nearly 30%. While this is low for the country, it is huge that this many people are without jobs. Countries with political turmoil like Gaza and the West Bank have 25% unemployment due to their political climates. Congo is at 20%. The lowest unemployment rate in modern history was Qatar at 0.1% unemployment. This is a rich country that depends on its natural resources, but it still cannot achieve zero. The truth is that no country can achieve it in the modern world.

Now that we have considered zero as a digit and as a word, let's look at some important principles before we move forward on our journey to adopt the "zero mindset".

1. First, we must **unlearn old habits** so we can start afresh. Easier said than done, especially when you grow older. As they say, "old habits die hard". Restarting in life is never easy, but it is necessary for change. I have learned in my long experience that it's better to fail fast than continuing to deny failure. It's certainly much cheaper to fail fast and learn from that mistake. We are creatures of habit, and one of those habits is denial, but one must become free to unlearn things that become unnecessary. Time and macro forces will often deal you an unexpected hand. The faster you respond, the better

you can overcome these surprises. Look at failure as a necessary evil. Great lessons are learned from it, and the greatest is when you overcome it.

2. **Understand the nature of number zero** to appreciate what it can do for you. I will look more at zero as both a digit and a word. They are equally important for your efficiency and mindset. Once you realize zero's powers, you become impervious to failure and will do better as you grow.

3. **Study its science and its mathematical mysteries!** We will look at what great mathematicians and scientists have taught us about zero. We will look at its philosophy and its mystery. We are only who we are from history; without what has been said or taught, we can never evolve. Once you understand the story of zero's creation, you will respect its power and more importantly learn how to take full advantage of its glow and charm. Division, multiplication, subtraction, or addition with zero makes it relevant to many new ideas that can be lessons in both your work and life. Zero is an evolution, and now I want you to think of it as your revolution.

4. Ask yourself, if all knowledge is now available, **can we reach zero errors?** Well, it's an impossible task: knowledge is expandable. Look at where artificial intelligence is taking us, a new era of simplicity that lies in complication. Knowledge

is available, but never the full knowledge. But it keeps getting better! Knowledge is growth itself; it expands and expands, like the universe. Just as nothing in life is complete, nothing in life is without error. If you could freeze time, there might be zero error, but when time is added, zero error expires!

5. In Chapter 6, *Media Rarities and Real-life Impacts*, we'll look at **climate change** and how the media doesn't play an active, daily role in addressing it. We were able to send humans to space, yet we can't seem to fix climate change. It's ironic that people can defy the seemingly impossible with travel, and yet they cannot adopt a way of life to save the planet. More importantly, why has this issue been buried to the public for decades, and why isn't there more focus on educating people about it?

6. **In life, you will often be puzzled**. This isn't a bad thing: Questioning is the essence of growth. If we don't question what's around us, we will accept where we are and stagnate. Being puzzled is natural, and it is important in life to challenge your thought and not automatically accept what is given to you. We should never take things for granted, just as we shouldn't take life itself for granted. When we set our alarm to wake tomorrow, we take it for granted that we will wake up. Or is it hope that allows us to plan for our future? Doesn't it puzzle you that we are absolutely certain we will wake up?

7. **I mean no offense**. I firmly believe that haters are only secret admirers in hiding. When we do something new or defy the obvious, we will be treated differently. That's not a bad thing. There are more negatives than positives in life and people can criticize faster than they can offer support. I was told once that developing a horror movie is much easier than a comedy. Remembering a joke is way harder than remembering misery.

8. Let's break the seriousness here and look at **things that don't make sense**, like pineapple on pizza. There are many things that don't make sense to me. I will chat about them, so you can find some happiness through laughter. Sometimes we see things that make us question why they're there. We do it in a funny way, perhaps, but it is important to point them out; it makes us more human. Most important, we must always be able to laugh at ourselves.

9. **Appreciate the art of nothing**, as it helps you develop an art of something. Silence, emptiness, calmness are all healthy. Meditation is powerful for the mind and soul. It is an art in itself. By meditating, you feel your own 'within', clearing your mind and soul to reach complete serenity and begin the process of acceptance.

10. **Acceptance is key!** Once we accept who we are and what we want to do, through belief and willpower, we see internal change and begin to implement that change externally. We

have all heard the saying that change is internal first. It begins with acceptance. Accept change within you and believe in it, so you can help others join the ride.

Together we will unleash the power of zero and become achievers.

Remember, when the clock hits 00:00, it's a new day, and more importantly, a new chance to start your growth. We move from a.m. to p.m. and p.m. to a.m., and we always add, never subtracting. I am not inventing this theory; I believe in its power and how it contributes to success. Every chapter is a step forward into accepting your own zero, where you defy possibilities and turn them into something better. We'll uncover more possibilities of the power of zero, but first, we must do some unlearning.

■ ■ ■

Countdown to Your Zero Mindset

1. **Power of adversity**: Facing hardship usually serves as a catalyst for extraordinary achievements, tapping into resilience, creativity, and determination.

2. **Variety of success paths**: Success doesn't always lead to fame; many achieve greatness quietly through resilience, innovation, and impactful contributions.

3. **Factors of success**: Resilience, innovation, impact, humility, timing, and fulfillment are key factors contributing to success, regardless of public recognition.

4. **Positive reframing of zero**: Zero represents opportunity, potential, and balance, challenging traditional views of success and failure.

5. **Embracing failure**: Failure can provide valuable insights and opportunities for growth, shaping individuals and fostering resilience.

6. **Reframing negatives**: Pairing "zero" with negatives highlights its transformative power, turning obstacles into opportunities for improvement.

7. **Role of unemployment**: Achieving zero unemployment remains a challenge globally, highlighting the complexity of societal and economic issues.

8. **Adopting the zero mindset**: Unlearning old habits, understanding the nature of zero, studying its science, questioning assumptions, and embracing challenges are crucial steps in adopting a "zero mindset".

9. **Challenging the status quo**: Embracing zero represents a rebellion against societal norms that glorify success

and stigmatize failure, fostering a culture of continuous improvement.

10. **Acceptance and growth**: Accepting one's faults and striving for continuous improvement unleashes the power of zero, driving personal and professional growth.

2

UNLEARN

"Recognize that un-learning is
the highest form of learning."

—Rumi

ONE OF THE hardest things I had to come to terms with, when I faced the challenge of my MBA and whenever I step into a new business venture, is the necessity of unlearning. Believe me, it's far from simple. Being in your forties and going back to academics is tricky, or at least it was to me.

Over time, I've collected a wealth of knowledge, both positive and negative, that lives within me. It's the sum of my experiences, shaping the lens through which I perceive the world.

When seeking answers, I often turn inward, drawing upon this pool of insights and lessons learned.

Acquiring new information is often straightforward. It can involve reading books, attending lectures, conducting research, or engaging in discussions with experts in a particular field. These activities deepen our understanding and broaden our knowledge base on a specific topic. Yet, the real significance lies in what happens next. Once new information is acquired, it doesn't exist in seclusion; instead, it interacts with and builds upon existing knowledge.

Imagine existing knowledge as a foundation, a solid base upon which new learnings are constructed. Just as a building relies on a solid foundation to support its structure, new knowledge relies on the framework provided by existing understanding. For example, let's say someone is learning about astronomy. They may start by learning the basics of the solar system, such as the names of planets and their orbits. As they go further into the subject, they build upon this foundational knowledge by exploring topics like cosmic mechanics, the life cycle of stars, and the formation of galaxies. Each new concept they encounter is understood and contextualized within the framework of what they already know.

In this way, existing knowledge acts as a podium, guiding the accumulation of new information and facilitating deeper understanding. It provides context, relevance, and connections that enhance the learning process. Without this foundation, new information may lack meaning, making it more challenging to grasp.

Building upon what we already know expands our horizons, makes new connections, and gives us deeper insights into the world around us.

I remember when I wanted to switch from squash to golf. It was very difficult for me, as my mind couldn't work on relaxing my right arm. I kept breaking clubs or hitting the grass all the time. Then I started playing golf left-handed, and it felt like I was starting something new, with no previous memory. My muscle memory didn't get confused and with practice I saw better results and started to enjoy it. I felt like I was ten years old again and learning a new game.

Unlearning feels like ripping yourself away from your current beliefs, because they no longer serve your future ambitions. It's challenging, but it is often essential for growth and progress. Do you remember when we were children? We learned fast because we had zero knowledge. So how to do it when you are an adult with all this knowledge and experience built up? You will get to appreciate the emptiness of a child's mind in the end!

Why Should We Unlearn?

I came across an insightful perspective from Richard Rohr: "Transformation is sometimes more about unlearning than learning." This process of unlearning minimizes the impact of outdated knowledge, paving the way for new possibilities. Futurist Alvin Toffler said that the illiterate of the 21st Century are not those who cannot read or write but rather those who cannot learn, unlearn, and relearn. But it's not easy. Unlearning isn't about forgetting what we already know; it's about acknowledging what we know and actively choosing a different way of looking at it. To unlearn means getting rid of old habits, old thinking, and whatever doesn't apply to your future. It can be challenging, but it's a vital part to moving forward.

Remember those old cassette players gathering dust somewhere? As technology developed, we had to learn how to use DVDs. Then we had to shift to the major streaming platforms we have today.

So, Why Unlearn?

Unlearning, learning, and relearning is a cycle representing the evolving nature of knowledge and skills in the modern world. Embedded in educational theory and practice, this cycle acknowledges that to stay relevant and adaptive, one must be willing to let go of outdated information, embody new knowledge, and continually refine our understanding.

Unlearning is crucial for several reasons, including adaptability and personal growth. As we navigate through different stages of life, the knowledge and behaviors that once served us well may become counterproductive. Unlearning biases and old habits while dismissing old ways of thinking are vital processes for making room for new perspectives and skills. Think of a human mind like a memory stick: The more you store, the less you can create space for new information. We need to prioritize holding on only to information that is crucial to current and future times.

Unlearning is Also Going Back to ZERO

The unlearning I am talking about is less about forgetting than the ability to choose a different approach or belief over an ingrained one that is no longer valuable. This is important in our rapidly changing world, where technological advancements and shifts in social norms can make old ways of doing things irrelevant. At the core, unlearning enables us to stay relevant, challenge our comfort zones, and grow throughout our lives. Don't worry, though: Unlearning doesn't mean forgetting what you have done; you simply start using different tactics and begin improving on your previous knowledge.

You must challenge your beliefs and question things to feel in control. This can be unsettling, but unlearning allows you to empty your cup, creating space for new information. Letting go is the most demanding part, as it often involves emotional investment and ego.

But don't feel bad. Remember, you get a chance to learn again! Learning allows you to adopt a mindset that is open to new experiences, perspectives, and information. It absorbs and actively engages information through reading, taking classes, conversations, and practical experience. The concept of unlearning forces you to be a critical thinker while evaluating new knowledge at a different pace. You will be able to determine its accuracy, relevance, and applicability, and this will help you incorporate the right new knowledge into your skillset and day-to-day activities.

Learning again, or "relearning", has significant psychological benefits. It reinforces neural pathways in the brain, enhancing memory and skill retention. Immersing yourself in relearning can increase cognitive flexibility, making it easier to adapt to new situations and solve problems in various contexts. Rethinking previously learned material or skills also promotes metacognition, "the ability to think about one's own thinking", which can result in more profound, more subtle understanding. This ongoing cycle of learning, unlearning, and relearning can foster a growth mindset, that is, a way of thinking that values effort, embraces challenges, and sees failure as an opportunity to learn. A simple example here would be learning a new language or perfecting your current language skills. Both will result in making you better.

The Backwards Bicycle Experiment

Destin Sandlin is an American engineer and science communicator. His experiment with the "backwards" bicycle offers valuable insights into neuroplasticity and the challenges of unlearning and relearning motor skills. Experiment participants struggle to adapt to reversed controls, showcasing the strength of existing neural pathways and the difficulty of overcoming ingrained habits. Cognitive dissonance is evident in the way individuals understand, intellectually, that things are reversed, yet continuously make mistakes due to muscle memory. The experiment emphasizes the importance of persistence and adaptation, as some participants eventually succeed in riding the backwards bicycle with practice. The amount of practice necessary may vary from person to person. For instance, while it took Sandlin eight months to learn to ride the backwards bike, it took his son only two *weeks*. Here we see the effects of neuroplasticity, which is the brain's ability to reorganize itself and adapt to new situations. Children have much greater neuroplasticity than adults, which is why it's easier for them to learn new skills and languages at an earlier age. The experiment also has broader implications for understanding the brain's adaptability to new technologies and skills. By demonstrating how difficult it is for an individual to unlearn and relearn a simple motor skill, such as riding a bicycle when the controls are reversed, Sandlin's experiment underscores the difficulty of overcoming ingrained habits and muscle memory. The challenge of adapting to the reversed controls felt by those with experience riding a regular bicycle emphasized how strong existing neural pathways can be.

Mental Flexibility is a Skill

The experiment showcases the cognitive dissonance that occurs when faced with conflicting information. Participants understand intellectually that the bicycle controls are reversed, but their instincts and muscle memory continually lead them to make mistakes. This illustrates the struggle between knowledge and ingrained habits. Sandlin's experiment highlights the importance of persistence and adaptation in the face of challenges. Over time, some participants manage to adapt and successfully ride the backwards bicycle, demonstrating the brain's ability to adjust and form new neural connections. With practice, one can unlearn and relearn skills one initially had.

From a growth perspective, relearning is a form of mental and skill 'upkeep' to be competitive and agile in your professional and personal endeavors. It allows you to update your knowledge and skills per current trends, technologies, and methodologies, thereby preventing stagnation. It can reignite passion and interest in a field, making you more engaged and productive. Moreover, relearning can help to identify gaps in one's understanding or skills, highlighting areas for further development or training. This adaptability is increasingly essential in today's fast-paced world, where the only constant is change.

As society evolves, there's a collective need to unlearn prejudices, stereotypes, and outdated practices, replacing them with more inclusive, equitable attitudes. I will give you an example from a professional standpoint. Relearning the latest programming languages could significantly impact your career evolution. In addition to being more competitive in the job market, you'll also be better positioned to contribute to projects at the cutting edge of technology. Your expanded skill set may open doors for you in specialized fields like artificial intelligence, machine learning, or data science.

You might also find renewed passion and enthusiasm for your work as you update and expand your skills, making you more engaged, productive, and open to future learning opportunities. Suppose you speak English and wish to learn Arabic or Japanese. The new language would require your mindset to shift from left to right or from horizontal to vertical and to engage with completely different letters and rules. As Sandlin pointed out in his backwards bike experiment, it is much easier for children to learn new languages, because their brains have more neuroplasticity and capacity to learn new things.

In both the psychological and professional senses, the process of relearning proves to be a valuable exercise. It prepares you for the continually evolving challenges in our frenetic environment, setting the stage for ongoing personal and professional development. The cycle of unlearning, learning, and relearning is a lifelong process and an essential aspect of personal and professional development. It allows individuals and organizations to remain agile, relevant, and better equipped to navigate the complexities of a constantly changing world.

In summary, there are three stages of growth (like a tree):

1. **Sapling stage** – Learning gives you potential.

2. **Shedding leaves** – Unlearning gives you a reason to move.

3. **Growing fully again** – Relearning opens new possibilities.

■ ■ ■

Countdown to Your Zero Mindset

1. **Unlearning for growth**: Unlearning old beliefs and habits is essential for personal and professional growth, even though it can be challenging, especially for adults with years of accumulated knowledge.

2. **Transformation through unlearning**: Transformation often involves unlearning outdated information or behaviors to make room for new possibilities and adapt to changing circumstances.

3. **The cycle of learning**: The process of unlearning, learning, and relearning is a lifelong cycle that fosters adaptability, cognitive flexibility, and continuous personal and professional development.

4. **Importance of relearning**: Relearning allows individuals to update their skills, stay relevant in their fields, and embrace new opportunities for growth and advancement.

5. **Neuroplasticity and adaptation**: Understanding neuroplasticity and the brain's ability to adapt to new situations highlights the importance of persistence and adaptation in unlearning and relearning skills, despite initial challenges.

6. **Leave room for something new**: It can be important sometimes to start from scratch and not build up from existing knowledge.

7. **Unlearn things to open up more space in your mind**: This is what allows new things to enter.

3

THE NATURE OF NUMBER ZERO

I'VE LONG BELIEVED that inactivity doesn't always equate to inaction; for some, it's a deliberate choice, a strategy to await the sensible moment. Yet, when we contemplate the number zero, its contradictory force and mysterious nature become apparent. Now, we'll explore what I call "the intro to growth: perfection in zero". When I started on this journey to uncover the number zero, I decided to discuss it with a close circle of friends. I was hoping to create a debate and collect different perspectives on the multiple topics surrounding the subject. I had mixed answers. Some wondered if there was any value at all in my project.

Most people took zero for granted; it was a given digit they had learned at a young age, one that goes with other numbers. Zero was forgotten as a stand-alone digit. I asked my friends: Why do you start with 1 when you count instead of 0? Was it a habit? Or is it because for you, zero represents nothingness? The answers came mostly in the form of a question: "Why would we need to start with zero in counting?" One even counted 1 to 10 on his fingers and joked, "Which finger represents zero?"

People were puzzled by my questions; they started to ridicule the number. I said, okay, now let me ask you where zero *does* make sense. They started to look at each other and define zero as a starting point, but only when you reach the number 10. Then I asked, "Where is 11 on your fingers?" just to inject a little humor into the topic, but I followed it with a serious question: "What does the number 10 mean?" That's when the discussion started to become interesting. I suggested we break the number 10 into 1 and 0. "Can we say that after the number nine we reach "One Zero", like 1 and 0 = 10? Is the number 20, Two Zero? Is the number 30, Three Zero, and so forth?" When I saw this get their attention, I said, "Now you see what zero does when we count: It creates the start of something bigger."

To uncover more of my perspective, let's understand what is happening around us today. People seem consumed with scaling things up, whether in business, personal lives, or technological advancements. Is this the right approach? This question troubled me as I developed my life and career, especially when I decided to build my own business. So, I asked myself over and over again: Why go bigger without fixing our core? It doesn't make sense that we cannot fix the negatives in what we do and yet expand anyway.

Is our mindset becoming one of greed, wanting more without deserving it, aiming for success without reaching zero error? Why is it so? Why are we inclined to seek magnitude over quality?

Is Success With Errors Still Success?

To me, this perspective is born out of desire and impatience, an urge to accumulate more without necessarily deserving it. It's a race to reach success without considering the possibility of a zero-error state or spending adequate time to rectify inherent issues. This approach undermines the whole purpose of growth, and you can't create a legacy in what you build while, deep down, there are faults.

The concept of zero defects, initially introduced by Philip Crosby in his 1985 book *Absolutes of Quality Management*, has gained widespread recognition in the field of quality management. It has become so influential that Six Sigma has incorporated it as a critical principle.[2] However, this idea has not been without

---

2   Six Sigma is a set of techniques and tools introduced in 1986 by engineer Bill Smith and used to improve business processes. Six Sigma practitioners use statistics, financial analysis, and project management to identify and reduce defects and errors, minimize variation, and increase quality and efficiency.

its share of criticism, with some arguing that achieving a state of zero defects is an impractical goal. Proponents contend that "zero defects" is not about attaining absolute perfection. Instead, it revolves around the elimination of waste, the reduction of defects, and the maintenance of the highest-quality standards in project execution.

The zero defects theory incorporates four vital elements for practical application in real projects.

1. Quality is an assurance aligned with requirements. Achieving zero defects in a project entails meeting the specified requirements at a given moment.

2. Embrace the "right the first time" approach. Quality should be seamlessly woven into the process from the outset, preventing the need for troubleshooting at later stages. As Philip D. Crosby says, "It is always cheaper to do the job right the first time."

3. Evaluate quality in financial terms. Assessing waste, production, and revenue in regard to their budgetary implications is essential.

4. Performance should be evaluated against accepted standards, aiming as close as possible to those standards.

Is the journey worthwhile? Let's shift gears, delve into the fascinating world of numbers, and figure this out together!

Zero is the Unsung Hero

In the mathematical world, the enigma, the paradox, the "nothing" means so much. In a funny way, zero is the life of the "math party", the guy who shows up with no snacks or drinks, just himself, a real "nothing-to-see-here" kind of character. Zero is like the ultimate wingman for other numbers. Add it to any number and the number stays the same, like a friend who never steals your spotlight. "You plus me equals you," zero says. How humble!

Do you remember the scene in *Seinfeld* (Season 5, episode 13, "The Dinner Party") where George Costanza argued that he shouldn't need to bring anything with him to a dinner party? He said that just bringing himself was enough! Bertrand Russell, who had a great deal of influence on mathematics, logic, set theory, and various areas of analytic philosophy, emphasized the foundational significance of zero in developing rigorous mathematical systems. Zero's introduction allows for creating a number line, providing a starting point for both positive and negative numbers. Moreover, zero becomes a pivotal concept in the context of limits and calculus.

Mathematicians leverage the idea of approaching zero to understand infinitesimal changes and rates of change, laying the groundwork for the calculus of derivatives and integrals. A mathematician of Russell's caliber would emphasize that zero is not merely a numerical placeholder but a cornerstone of mathematical structure, enabling the development of advanced concepts and systems. Its presence and properties influence everything from basic arithmetic to calculus and set theory complexities.

Yet, zero has its boundaries, its non-negotiables. Zero refuses to be the denominator, for example, asserting its enigmatic status.

> "The time you enjoy wasting is not wasted time."
>
> —Bertrand Russell

Multiply zero by any number, and BOOM! Everything turns into a zero. It's always ready to reject anything it multiplies with, like a magician whose only trick is making things disappear. One minute, you envision a hat full of options, and then nothing is there, zero.

But wait, there's a plot twist! Zero is also the diva of the mathematical world, refusing division by any other number. Talk about being high-maintenance! If zero were to be personified, they would likely be a figure of balance, potential, and infinite possibilities, guiding others towards a deeper understanding of themselves and the world around them. Zero is a master of self-deprecation: They wouldn't take themselves too seriously and would often poke fun at their own "zero-ness". They might joke about being the "underdog" or the "bottom of the barrel", turning their supposed shortcomings into comedic fodder.

Zero may look like "nothing", but it's the secret agent, game-changer, and ultimate sidekick in the numbers world. Don't let that blank, round face fool you: Zero's got some superpowers!

Zero and Logic

Life sometimes creates moments that defy reason. From bizarre fashion trends to confusing conspiracy theories, we often find ourselves in situations that are difficult to comprehend—they make zero sense. On the other hand, there are positive things that make zero sense, too. For example, advancements in Artificial Intelligence (AI) come to life by data, and lots of it. At the core of machine learning algorithms lies the mighty but straightforward zero, acting as the binary opposite of one, enabling complex computations and predictions.

This is a case where zero amplifies sense rather than diminishing it, a robust number and a tool to eliminate the negatives! But if a number slightly off zero may seem insignificant in isolation, its effects can be magnified, depending on the context and the precision required in the application. It underscores the importance of attention to detail and the potential consequences of even the smallest deviation in numerical values. Having 0.2% of something doesn't seem like a lot. But if that "something" is one billion dollars, we're talking about two million dollars! As in an interest rate, if there is an extra hidden decimal while calculating the result, you might lose more if that extra digit after the decimal is not taken into consideration.

If Zero Decided to Take a Vacation from the Digits

What do you think would happen if zero took a vacation? I believe chaos would ensue in the numerical world! Without zero, the other digits would throw a wild party, but nobody would know where to stand! Numbers would be jumbling around without any order on the dancefloor.

If there were no zero, mathematicians would be scratching their heads trying to figure out how to do basic arithmetic. Adding, subtracting, multiplying, and dividing would become like solving a Rubik's Cube blindfolded: confusing and full of mistakes! Writing numbers would become a game of charades. Imagine trying to write down your phone number without the glorious zero! It would look something like a scrambled mess. Good luck trying to call anyone! And adding plus wouldn't work, as no one would know that the "+" in an international number actually requires the dialing of two zeros. (For example, when you make international calls, you add 00 before the phone number.)

What about the zero in computers? Zero is a best friend in the binary world, representing "off" or "not there". Without it, they'd be lost in a sea of confusion, crashing and burning like a robot caught in a paradox. In short, life without zero would be like trying to navigate a maze blindfolded while riding a unicycle: hilarious for bystanders, but an absolute disaster for anyone trying to make sense of numbers!

Most of us consume social media of some kind. You'll recognize the positive and ambitious crowd we see while scrolling. They push us to "increase" or "make better", whether it's wealth, travel, fun, or love. In my opinion, the other urge, the one to decrease, while much rarer, is a bit wiser: to reach zero crime, zero waste, zero health issues, zero hate. Isn't this the way we should make things better?

When was the last time you experienced zero issues? A utopian deal! Probably never. But that doesn't stop us from aspiring to a world where problems are minimal. I hope that AI, powered by the binary language of zeros and ones, may help us realize this aspiration by identifying and solving problems before they escalate, thus bringing us closer to a state of "zero issues".

So, if we aspire to eliminate the negatives, isn't that perfection itself?

Remembering that some things may never reach complete "zero" is vital. Aspiring for improvement and reducing negatives is a goal that can be enabled by leveraging technologies. For instance, a person might catch the COVID-19 virus but be lucky enough to experience zero symptoms. According to *Medical News Today*, around 4 in 10 people who catch the virus don't experience symptoms! This virus shocked the world and became the main topic of everyone's life, but COVID was only scary with symptoms; without symptoms, nothing happened. It was a sad period of human loss and fatality, my condolences to the families and friends who had to suffer.

Zero is a more significant number than you think!

It's more than just a number; it's a concept, a goal, a catalyst, and much more. Zero is a fascinating subject worthy of deeper exploration, from its mathematical properties to its philosophical implications and role in emerging technologies.

As we continue navigating our lives, let's remember that sometimes the answers we seek lie in the domain of "nothingness" that zero represents. Sometimes, it is the most significant number of them all.

This chapter scratched the surface of zero; the journey to understanding zero is like diving into an endless abyss; it offers a picture of possibilities, each more intriguing than the last. It's high time we gave zero the credit it deserves, not just as a number but as a symbol that shapes our understanding of the world in more ways than we could ever imagine.

To dwell on this more, let's go back in time and examine the mathematical science behind zero in the next chapter.

■ ■ ■

Countdown to Your Zero Mindset

1. **Reevaluation of zero**: Exploring the concept of zero stimulates a reevaluation of its significance beyond its traditional role as a starting point in counting.

2. **Perspective on zero**: Through discussions with friends, different perspectives on zero emerge, from its role as a mere starting point to its potential as a catalyst for growth and change.

3. **Questioning traditional approaches**: The discussion challenges traditional counting approaches and highlights zero's importance in understanding larger numerical systems.

4. **Growth and perfection**: The concept of "zero defects" in quality management underscores the pursuit of perfection

and quality, challenging the modern mindset of prioritizing magnitude over quality.

5. **Zero's mathematical significance**: Zero's role in mathematics was explored, from its foundational significance in creating number lines to its role in calculus and set theory.

6. **Zero's unique properties**: Zero's unique properties in arithmetic, multiplication, and division were highlighted, showcasing its importance and impact on numerical operations.

7. **Zero's symbolic meaning**: Beyond its numerical value, zero represents balance, potential, and infinite possibilities, influencing mathematical structures and calculations.

8. **Zero's impact on artificial intelligence**: In AI and machine learning, zero is a binary opposite, enabling complex computations and predictions.

9. **Hypothetical scenario without zero**: Imagining a world without zero reveals the chaos and confusion in numerical notation and calculations.

10. **Aspiration for zero**: Aspiring for a world with minimal negatives and striving towards "zero issues" is seen as an ideological goal that can be facilitated by leveraging technology and practical expectations.

4

MATHEMATICAL MYSTERIES

WHEN WE START to understand zero, it's essential to look at its mathematics, its properties, and how it has impacted science and math. As a number before one or after minus one, it separates the negative from the positive. It's quite simple when you look at it this way, but imagine zero wasn't created as a stand-alone, and we went from minus to plus directly; that doesn't make sense, right?

Let's try to make zero's properties a bit more light-hearted.

Zero is like the ultimate party crasher. You can add it to any number, and it's as if it was never there! It's the ultimate "plus one" that doesn't change the party's vibe. I am sure you've all been there, seeing a guest with a plus one and that person is irrelevant to the party crowd. When zero gets involved in multiplication, it's like performing a magic trick where everything disappears! You can multiply any number by zero, and poof! It all goes away, leaving behind a big fat zero.

Let's call it the vanishing zero.

Zero has an identity crisis; it's always trying to blend in. Add zero to any number, and it just tries to fit in like it's always been there. It's the chameleon of the number world. Another example that comes to mind is the sponge! Think of zero as the sponge in the kitchen sink of mathematics. Throw any number at it for multiplication, and zero soaks it all up, leaving everything dripping wet with … you guessed it, zero!

Ah, division by zero, the forbidden fruit of mathematics. It's like trying to divide a pizza by zero slices. You can try, but you'll end up with a mess and a confused look.

In summary, zero may seem like the shy kid at the number party, but it's secretly pulling off some pretty cool tricks and causing mischief along the way!

Zero is an unknown at the intersection of philosophy, religion, and mathematics. It's a simple concept that a child can understand, yet so complex that it has been the subject of strict mathematical inquiry for centuries.

When something is neither positive nor negative, it gets confusing. Is it the absence of a negative, or positive? I feel more inclined towards zero as a positive than as a negative. If I lose something, it's negative; if I don't lose something, it's what? The status quo? Or maybe something positive?

Do you remember this theory: Is the glass half-full or half-empty? It is a mindset that refers to a person's perspective on a situation, mainly when confronted with challenges. It is often used as a metaphor to illustrate two opposing attitudes towards life, one for optimism and the other for pessimism. Neither perspective is naturally right or wrong, but they can significantly impact one's overall wellbeing in the face of adversity.

Think of it like a balance: You can't be negative or positive without zero! One way to see it is that it defines equilibrium: When things are settled, they become transparent and fresh. A new start can only apply when you begin from zero, with no baggage from before and a clear perspective.

The history of the number zero is a fascinating journey that takes us across cultures, mathematical theories, and philosophies. This simple yet profound concept has roots in ancient civilizations and has travelled through time to become an essential element of modern mathematics, science, and technology.

Let's look at some examples in history and take ourselves back in time to uncover some of its mysteries.

Mesopotamia: The Cradle of Placeholder Zero

The concept of zero, or something like it, first appeared in Mesopotamia around 300 B.C. The Sumerians, and later the Babylonians, used a positional number system but initially had no symbol for zero. They used a two-dimensional space as a placeholder to signify a gap in the numbers. This early form of zero wasn't the number we know today, but rather a practical mechanism to distinguish between numbers like (for example) 31 from 301.

Ancient India: Zero Earns its Place

Zero received more comprehensive treatment in ancient India as both a concept and a numeral. Around 628 A.D., the Indian mathematician and astronomer Brahmagupta provided regulations for calculations involving zero and its operations. He defined zero for the first time as a number and not just a placeholder, transforming it from a grammatical abnormality into an arithmetic enabler. It is closely tied to cultural, philosophical, and mathematical developments during that period. The concept of "nothingness" or "void" wasn't new in a society deeply rooted in intellectual discourse. What was groundbreaking was how this philosophical idea was normalized into a mathematical concept that could be worked with in a systematic way.

Brahmagupta's work was part of a larger text called *Brahmasphuta-siddhanta*, in which he covered various aspects of arithmetic, geometry, and trigonometry. Brahmagupta described zero for division, which helped set the stage for algebra. Brahmagupta stated that adding or subtracting a zero from a number leaves the number unchanged and that multiplying a number by zero results in zero. However, one of the most controversial aspects was dividing by zero, which Brahmagupta described as yielding infinity, a concept that would later receive more formal scrutiny. While the notion of dividing by zero is still undefined in modern mathematics, Brahmagupta's attempt to tackle it was groundbreaking for his time.

Philosophical Reinforcements

The cultural and philosophical beliefs of ancient India likely played a role in zero's development as well. Concepts related to "nothingness" and the "void" had been discussed in Indian philosophical texts and had religious connotations. In early Buddhism, the idea of *Shunyata* (emptiness, void-ness) is crucial. Likewise, in Hindu cosmology, the view of a cyclic universe that goes through phases of creation (*srishti*) and dissolution (*pralaya*) gave the intellectual flexibility needed to contemplate the concept of "nothing" or "zero".

Zero was not just an isolated discovery but a part of the development of the decimal number system in India, which also contained place value. This was a tremendous shift in how calculations could be carried out, enabling more accessible and efficient measures. This number system was picked up by Islamic scholars in the 8th Century, and the concept began spreading widely.

Spreading the Concept (8th to 14th Centuries)

The second generation of the number zero occurred when Brahmagupta's work, along with other Indian mathematical treatises, was translated into Arabic. These texts played a vital role in spreading the concept of zero and the Indian number system during the Islamic Golden Age, establishing the foundation for today's numerical system.

This was a period of extraordinary intellectual activity in the Middle East, North Africa, and parts of Europe under Islamic rule. During this period, scholars in Islamic learning centers made significant advances in medicine, astronomy, mathematics, and philosophy. These scholars also played a crucial role in preserving and transmitting ancient knowledge, including that of ancient Greece, Rome, and India.

Major cities like Baghdad, Córdoba, and Cairo became centers of learning and culture, attracting scholars from various parts of the world. One of the most significant contributions of this period was the translation of important Greek, Latin, and Sanskrit works into Arabic. The Bayt al-Hikma (House of Wisdom) in Baghdad was a notable example of such a center, where Greek and Roman works were translated alongside original research.

Al-Khwarizmi, an Islamic scholar, who was the head of the house of wisdom in Baghdad in the 9th Century, wrote his seminal work *Al-Kitab al-Mukhtasar fi Hisab al-Jabr wal-Muqabala* (*The Compendious Book on Calculation by Completion and Balancing*), which not only introduced the Indian system of numerals (what we often refer to as "Arabic numerals" today) but also laid down foundational principles for algebra. Al-Khwarizmi's work included rules for working with the number zero, a concept previously not used in Western mathematical thinking. This profoundly impacted the development of mathematics.

The adoption of zero and the decimal system was groundbreaking for multiple reasons. It allowed for more straightforward and accurate calculations, which were essential for fields like astronomy, engineering, and finance. The concept of zero was crucial in developing algorithms and, later, algorithmic thinking, which is the basis of today's computer science. Moreover, it had philosophical implications, creating room for conceptual thought in mathematics and sciences.

In medicine, the measurements needed for determining dosages and time intervals were also made easier with the adoption of zero and the decimal system; and in astronomy, complex calculations involving the movement of cosmic bodies became more manageable. Al-Battani, Al-Farabi of the 10th Century, and many other astronomers and scientists could only have contributed the advancements they made with the mathematical tools introduced during this period.

In summary, the Islamic Golden Age was instrumental in spreading the concept of zero and other advanced mathematical ideas from India to the Islamic world and eventually to Europe. This was not just a transfer of knowledge but an augmentation of it. The Arabic scholars translated these works and added to them, setting the stage for the later European Scientific Revolution. The conceptual leaps made during this period, particularly concerning the number zero, were crucial milestones in human thought, fundamentally transforming how we understand the world.

Toward Europe

By the end of the Islamic Golden Age, Europe was beginning to emerge from its Dark Ages. It was an era of resistance and acceptance. Twelfth-century translations of Arabic works into Latin, often by scholars in Spain, included the Arabic numerical system and algebra. This transformed science, technology, and trade, leading to the European Renaissance.

Europe was initially resistant to the idea of zero, partly due to the abacus-based calculation system and partly because of the philosophical and religious implications of "nothingness". However, the concept started gaining acceptance with the translation of Arabic texts into Latin. By the late Middle Ages, zero was an integral part of the Arabic numeral system, which replaced the Roman numeral system for scientific calculations.

As the scientific revolution gathered pace, the concept of zero began to take its place in calculus and fundamental number theory. Mathematicians like Isaac Newton and Gottfried Wilhelm Leibniz used zero in their groundbreaking work. Zero is an essential building block of mathematics and science today, enabling us to express everything from zero-point energy in quantum mechanics to the coordinates on a digital map.

Philosophical and Cultural Interpretations

Zero has also been subject to various philosophical and cultural interpretations. It's been seen as a symbol of the void, non-being, and infinity. In Eastern philosophies, the concept of "nothingness" is often treated with more nuance and has been seen as a point of departure for deeper philosophical or spiritual inquiry.

In today's digital world, zero has taken on a new role as one of the two fundamental elements of binary code (the other being one), which forms the basis of virtually all modern computing systems. Thus, the origins and evolution of the number zero offer a fascinating glimpse into the history of human thought. From its humble beginnings as a placeholder in ancient scripts to its foundational role in modern mathematics and computing, zero is much more than "nothing". It's a testament to human ingenuity and the ever-evolving nature of our understanding of the world.

Zero in Sports

In many sports, you don't see jerseys with the number zero; as a matter of fact, in NFL the number zero is actually banned for players. This is because there is no position in the game defined by zero. It's neither defense nor offence.

Similarly, in racket sports such as tennis, padel tennis, and badminton, the term "zero" is often referred to as "love". This could be an expression of playing for the love of the game and sportsmanship. Another theory is that "love" originates from the French word "l'oeuf", which means "egg" and resembles the shape of zero. Over time, "l'oeuf" might have been anglicized to "love", contributing to its current usage in these sports.

Place Value System

Zero is essential in our place value system. Its role as a placeholder makes it possible to distinguish between numbers like 10 and 100 or 5 and 50. Without zero, our numerical system would be unmanageable. Consider the number 102. The zero in the ten's place indicates that there are no tens, thus making it clear that the number is one hundred and two, not ten and two or one and two. Similarly, in the number 50, the zero signifies no tens, making it fifty rather than five.

Cryptography

Zero-knowledge proofs are an essential concept in modern cryptography. They are used in cryptographic protocols to verify the authenticity of information without exposing sensitive data. For example, in password authentication systems, a user can prove to a server that they know the password without revealing the password itself. In blockchain and digital currency, zero-knowledge proofs are utilized to enhance privacy and confidentiality in transactions. For instance in 2012, Dr Alessandro Chiesa, an expert in cryptography, complexity theory, and computer security, developed the zk-SNARK protocol (Zero-Knowledge Succinct Non-Interactive Arguments of Knowledge) to allow transactions to be verified on a blockchain without revealing the sender, receiver, or transaction amount. This ensures that data sharing is sensitive and protocols are made available without disclosing the underlying data; it also has applications in fields such as healthcare, where patient data privacy is paramount.

Overall, zero-knowledge concepts offer powerful tools for enhancing security, privacy, and trust in various digital interactions, making them invaluable in fields where confidentiality and authenticity are paramount.

Zero-sum Game

In game theory, zero is at the heart of zero-sum games, where one player's gain is another player's loss. The best example of a zero-sum game is a game of poker between friends; the amount of money won by one player is lost by another. The total money in the game stays the same; it's just redistributed among the players. In a simple two-candidate election, any vote for one candidate is not going to the other. The positions are mutually exclusive, as only one candidate can win.

To conclude this historical trip into origin of zero: Brahmagupta's work encapsulates a leap in conceptual thinking. An ancient philosophical concept found formal representation in a system of numbers and rules that would become integral to modern mathematics. The Indian numeral and mathematical system, of which zero was an indispensable part, moved via Islamic scholarship into Europe, altering the scientific landscape permanently. Even today, zero remains a cornerstone of calculus, number theory, and every scientific endeavor involving mathematics.

In many ways, zero is the keystone of our intellectual endeavors, a symbol of the limits of human experience and the vastness of our potential for discovery. But the mystery of zero is far from solved.

■ ■ ■

Countdown to Your Zero Mindset

1. **Zero's mathematical impact**: Zero, an abstract concept, has profoundly impacted mathematics and science, serving as a fundamental element in various calculations and systems.

2. **Light-hearted analogies**: We've likened zero's personality to those of a party crasher, a chameleon, and a sponge in the world of numbers.

3. **Philosophical and cultural significance**: Zero's philosophical and cultural interpretations, including its association with "nothingness" and "infinity", have shaped its understanding in different societies.

4. **Historical development**: From its origins in Mesopotamia to its comprehensive treatment in ancient India, zero's historical development can be traced through key figures like Brahmagupta and Al-Khwarizmi.

5. **Spread through the Islamic Golden Age**: The Islamic Golden Age played a crucial role in spreading the concept of zero and the Indian numeral system, leading to advancements in various fields of study.

6. **Acceptance in Europe**: Despite initial resistance, zero gained acceptance in Europe during the Middle Ages, catalyzing the Renaissance and transforming scientific and mathematical thinking.

7. **Modern relevance**: Zero's place in modern mathematics, science, and technology is central.

8. **Place value system**: Zero's role as a placeholder in the place value system is crucial for distinguishing between numbers and facilitating efficient calculations.

9. **Cryptography and game theory**: Zero's significance in cryptography and game theory demonstrates its application in ensuring security, privacy, and strategic decision-making.

10. **Continued mystery**: Despite centuries of study, zero remains a mysterious and profound concept, challenging our understanding of mathematics, logic, and reality. Its historical development and cultural interpretations reflect the ongoing quest to unravel its mysteries.

5

IF ALL KNOWLEDGE IS AVAILABLE

Even in an era of accessibility of knowledge, innovation remains essential.

TODAY, TECHNOLOGY HAS brought a wealth of information to our fingertips, and the possibilities seem limitless. But it's crucial to recognize that true progress lies not only in having knowledge, but also in harnessing it to address the fundamental questions and challenges that define our existence.

How is zero essential in this quest? Let's think about knowledge and how we use it.

Application of Things

Innovation emerges from new knowledge or from applying existing knowledge in unique ways or contemporary contexts. Among other sources, our knowledge can come from firsthand experiences or from what we have witnessed from others. In most cases, our choices are based on our experiences, but knowing if they are right or wrong will only come *after* we choose! We can only make decisions based on what we know today. Later on, we might be able to make different decisions based on new information. Does that make all decisions change with time, or are some decisions always right? If we have zero knowledge, how can we apply what we have learned? By mixing different subjects, you can learn things you wouldn't be able to understand if you just studied one issue alone. Interconnected approaches can result in impossible innovations within a single field.

For instance, bioinformatics combines biology and computer science to derive new insights and tools. Bioinformatics is an interdisciplinary field that combines biology, computer science, mathematics, and statistics to analyze and interpret biological data, particularly large datasets generated from biological experiments. The field emerged in response to the vast amount of biological information produced by advancements in molecular biology, genomics, and other related disciplines.

Imagine you're a kid again, and you're trying to figure out why your friend spends their allowance on video games instead of saving it. You might ask your parents or a teacher how money works to understand this better. That's using economics.

But what if you could also understand what's happening in your friend's brain when they decide to buy a game? What makes it so exciting for them? That's where brain science, or neuroscience, comes in. Imagine mixing the "money stuff" with the "brain stuff" to understand why people make confident choices. When you combine those things, you get something called "Neuroeconomics". It helps us understand what people do and why they do it by looking at both money and the brain simultaneously.

New Problems Emerge

As society evolves, new challenges arise. These challenges demand innovative solutions, even if we have vast amounts of existing knowledge. It's simply a part of our reality that with every step we take forward, we see more problems to fix. This brings us to a new kind of unknown: There will be mysteries that we can only tackle when we reach them.

Whether I was building my own company or working for someone else, I often came up with new ideas. They made sense to me, but making them relatable to others required in-depth study and, more importantly, becoming a solution provider. The best way to explain new ideas is to make them relatable and simple. You always need to define a problem before you seek a solution: Find it so you can fix it. So, if you are looking to sell a product online, present your advertising in a way that targets the right audience and answers a question your customers have or serves a need.

Once you establish an idea, you need to go back to zero to find the real value in it.

Personal Perspectives

Individuals interpret knowledge based on their experiences, backgrounds, and cultural contexts. This diversity of thought is a breeding ground for innovation. It's funny how our perspectives are reached today. Imagine we were all born this year with its technology. Do you think we would have more cultural differences, or would our actions be more similar? What we have learned or created affects the fundamentals that change us in our lifetime. If we never started anything new, we would all be similar. It's because we make changes, because we start new things, that we created differences.

Moving forward is creating more change.

To get people to buy into your new concept or product, you need to narrow down the similarities of ideas that could resonate easily with others: Find common ground between what you're selling or presenting so your audience feels you are talking their language. Communication is key. When you set the proper tone, you can address any issue clearly. Thus everyone feels connected to the same idea, and by collaborative thought you can come to a better conclusion. We all experience disconnection when someone speaks only from within their own mind. Thought that only *you* can relate to is not communication.

This is when you go back to zero. Before you assume a tone to your communication, understand the setting you are in and the people around you and start from a place where you will be understood.

Technological Advancements

As technology evolves, it provides new tools and platforms for further innovation. What was complicated a few years ago will be more straightforward in the future. Yet we will have more new things, with more innovation. Where does this end? Or are we stuck in an infinite loop of growth and change? Can we ever go back to "zero", or is this an impossible task? We are yet to find out. Artificial Intelligence is becoming powerful. Combined with the human brain, it will bring about powerful change!

Limitations Inspire Creativity

Sometimes constraints, whether they be physical, economic, or societal, can push people to think outside the box. My first experience with this was early in my career in advertising, in late 1990s Saudi Arabia. There were many government restrictions and rules to abide by to advertise anything. We weren't even allowed to advertise faces, and it was always necessary to use a kind of double language. Most of the employees were expats, so we never got it right from the first attempt. But in this type of situation, a challenge can also be an exciting way to test our imagination. Your mind must be wired back to zero to start thinking of how to be creative in a completely new way. Then you begin to understand how to do it again by having adapted to constraints the first time. Still, it was a mental challenge to many of these creative people: How often can we wire our minds to restart from zero?

Continuous Improvement

Even if a problem has a solution, there's always room for improvement. Innovators constantly tweak existing solutions to make them better, faster, or more efficient. It has been said that Thomas Edison tried more than 2700 light bulbs before getting it right. By now, you'd think that technology would allow us to create a bulletproof solution from the first attempt, right? But we find ourselves having to go back to zero again and again.

Zero is becoming more sensible now, the start of creation and re-creation!

New Knowledge is Born from Old

In ancient times, zero was avoided because it was equated with 'nothingness'. However, as we have seen, when mathematicians and philosophers began to explore its properties, zero went from being nothing to being a crucial element to describe everything from black holes to the behavior of algorithms in a computer program. It became a line of thought for entirely new mathematical languages, theories, and technologies that weren't possible without it.

Scholars expanded zero's utility across different disciplines by examining its nature. This is a perfect example of how interrogating existing knowledge can lead to new avenues of inquiry and revolutionary insights. In a world where seemingly all knowledge is accessible, questioning becomes even more important, as it paves the way for innovation and discovery.

Cultural and Societal Shifts

Shifts in cultural and societal values often act as catalysts for re-evaluating what we know and propelling us toward new frontiers of knowledge and innovation. When a society collectively values something new, like sustainability, that priority influences various activities, from government policy on renewable energy to individual behavior.

Look at societal and cultural shifts toward greater inclusivity and diversity. They have forced the re-evaluation of existing practices across various sectors, leading to innovation in areas that might not have been obvious before. The push for inclusivity in the technology domain has led to the development of more accessible products and services. Features like voice-activated virtual assistants, screen readers, and compatible devices have become more commonplace, not as specialized products but as integrated features. The drive to be more inclusive has required designers and developers to rethink the user experience, making technology accessible to everyone regardless of physical or cognitive ability.

The call for greater representation in the media and entertainment industry has led to a broader range of stories being told, from different cultural perspectives and sexual orientations. This enriches the storytelling landscape, opening up new markets and audiences, making it an innovation in both a social and a business sense. Similarly, in education, there has been a move toward more inclusive curricula that represent a greater range of histories and viewpoints. This fosters a more comprehensive educational experience and prepares students for a globalized world.

Questioning the status quo is vital in a world of shifting societal values. Doing so also fosters innovation and updates existing knowledge and practices. We can think of this as a process of perpetually beginning again, and where better to begin again than from zero?

Emphasis on Experience

Beyond just solving problems, businesses have to focus on enhancing users' experiences. Design thinking, which emphasizes empathy with users, can lead to innovative products and services that offer better user experiences.

In essence, while having access to all knowledge provides a foundation, it's the human capacity for creativity, our ever-evolving challenges, and our diverse ways of interpreting and applying knowledge that drives innovation.

I was always in favor of coming to a conclusion on my own, without any external force or knowledge. This was what defined my personal creativity. But this can be very limiting; specifically, you are limited to what you have observed in life! It's better to get external support so that when you start from zero you have a wider perspective. When we create for an audience wider than ourselves, we need to be more diverse in our thoughts and ideas. Knowing something and applying it are two different things.

■ ■ ■

Countdown to Your Zero Mindset

1. **Harnessing knowledge**: In today's era of accessibility, true progress lies not just in having knowledge, but in applying it to address fundamental questions and challenges.

2. **Interdisciplinary innovation**: Combining knowledge from different fields leads to innovation; examples include bioinformatics, neuroeconomics, and interdisciplinary problem-solving.

3. **New challenges, new solutions**: As society evolves, new challenges arise, demanding innovative solutions even with existing knowledge.

4. **Continuous improvement**: Innovators tweak existing solutions to make them better, faster, or more efficient, leading to continuous improvement over time.

5. **Zero as a starting point**: Going back to zero allows for re-evaluation and improvement of ideas, sparking creativity and innovation.

6. **Cultural and societal shifts**: Changes in societal values prompt re-evaluation of existing knowledge, fostering innovation in areas like sustainability, inclusivity, and diversity.

7. **User experience emphasis**: Design thinking and emphasis on user experience drives innovation in products and services, enhancing overall usability and satisfaction.

8. **Human creativity**: While knowledge provides a foundation, human creativity and diverse interpretations drive innovation forward.

9. **Application of knowledge**: Knowing something is different from applying it; the foundation of knowledge lies in its practical application to solve real-world problems and improve human experiences.

6

MEDIA RARITIES AND REAL-LIFE IMPACTS

What is salient is not important.
What is important is not salient.

THIS WAS THE opening line of George Monbiot's piece in the *Guardian* in September 2022 called "Earth is Under Threat, Yet You Would Scarcely Know It". The statement means that the media confuses what is not important for what is, and vice versa!

Climate change is among the most critical issues of our time, with consequences impacting the environment and human societies, economies, and global stability. Yet, public perception of climate change can often be fragmented, inconsistent, or ill-informed, worsened by media coverage or a lack of information. Monbiot's reflection sheds light on the complex relationship between climate change and media, evaluating how media shapes perceptions, challenges, and the potential for significant impact.

Let's look at the concepts of "net zero" and "1.5 degrees Celsius warming" and their implications for the Earth:

In its Fifth Assessment Report, released in 2018, the Intergovernmental Panel on Climate Change (IPCC) provided scientific input into the Paris Agreement. The Agreement aims to strengthen the global response to the threat of climate change by holding the increase in the global average temperature to well below 2ºC above pre-industrial levels and to pursue efforts to limit the temperature increase to 1.5ºC above pre-industrial levels.

Net zero refers to achieving a balance between the amount of greenhouse gases (GHGs) emitted into the atmosphere and the amount removed or offset through various means such as carbon capture and storage, emissions reductions, and afforestation. Afforestation is the process of establishing forests on land that has not been forested for a significant period or has never been forested before. It involves planting trees or seeds and nurturing their growth to create new forested areas.

The goal of achieving net zero emissions is crucial in combating climate change. By stabilizing the concentration of GHGs in the atmosphere, we can mitigate the adverse effects of global warming, such as rising temperatures, extreme weather events, sea level rise, and loss of biodiversity.

Achieving net zero emissions requires significant changes in energy production, transportation, agriculture, and other sectors of the economy. It involves transitioning to renewable energy sources, improving energy efficiency, implementing carbon pricing mechanisms, and adopting sustainable land use practices. It involves innovation and eliminating the negatives. In short, it requires a zero mindset.

1.5 Degrees Celsius Warming

The Paris Agreement, a treaty according to international law, was adopted in 2015. Its target of limiting global warming to well below 2 degrees Celsius above pre-industrial levels is based on scientific evidence indicating that exceeding 1.5 degrees Celsius of warming could have severe and irreversible consequences for the planet.

Limiting warming to 1.5 degrees Celsius would reduce the risk of catastrophic impacts, such as more frequent and intense heatwaves, droughts, hurricanes, and wildfires. It would also help preserve vulnerable ecosystems, such as coral reefs, Arctic sea ice, and tropical forests, which provide essential services and support biodiversity.

However, achieving the 1.5 degrees Celsius target requires rapid and far-reaching transitions across all sectors of society.

It necessitates more ambitious emissions reductions, increased investment in renewable energy and low-carbon technologies, and enhanced international cooperation to address climate change effectively.

Failing to achieve net zero emissions and exceeding 1.5 degrees Celsius of warming would have profound and widespread consequences for the Earth's climate system, ecosystems, and human societies. Increased temperatures would exacerbate heat-related illnesses, food and water shortages, and displacement of populations due to sea level rise and extreme weather events. Vulnerable communities, particularly in developing countries, would bear the brunt of these impacts.

Biodiversity loss would also accelerate, leading to species extinctions and disruptions to ecosystem services essential for human wellbeing, such as pollination, water purification, and carbon sequestration.

Limiting global warming to 1.5 degrees Celsius and achieving net zero emissions offers a way to avoid the most severe impacts of climate change, protect vulnerable ecosystems, and build a more sustainable and resilient future for generations to come.

In summary, the concepts of net zero emissions and limiting global warming to 1.5 degrees Celsius are interconnected goals that require urgent and concerted action to address the climate crisis and safeguard the health and stability of the Earth's systems.

The media plays an unusual role in informing the public and shaping its opinion. Newspapers, television, and more recently, social media are the primary channels for conveying information to the masses. In the case of climate change, the media has the power to elevate its voice, turning conceptual data into compelling stories that resonate with the public. Let's call it content that matters in a way that can be understood.

Consistent, accurate, and high-visibility reporting makes people more likely to perceive climate change as a genuine threat requiring immediate action. Likewise, media can create role models, showcase success stories, and facilitate public engagement by translating the complicated language of scientific reports into easily understandable terms.

Media plays a pivotal role in prioritizing climate change, as emphasized by experts in the media industry and psychologists. The issue is that media seems to take zero responsibility for sharing information, and therefore zero information is shared. Look at the news: Nothing towards climate change is prioritized, unless it is supported by a commercial or an event.

Esteemed journalists and industry leaders acknowledge their responsibility for accurately representing climate change issues, emphasizing storytelling to engage audiences, and promoting public awareness and accountability. They stress the importance of framing and messaging that resonate with individuals' values and emotions, encouraging a sense of urgency and highlighting potential solutions. Psychologists additionally highlight the significance of reducing the perceived psychological distance of climate change, utilizing trusted messengers, and incorporating emotional appeals to evoke empathy, concern, or hope. Both groups underscore the need for media to address psychological barriers, such as perceived helplessness, and to showcase positive portrayals of sustainable behaviors that influence social norms.

Reaching net zero is a primary goal of environmental justice, which refers to "the fair treatment and meaningful involvement of all people, regardless of race, color, national origin, or income, in the development, implementation, and enforcement of environmental laws, regulations and policies."[3] Environmental justice also has the goal of ensuring that the burden of transition does not fall disproportionately on marginalized communities. But how does the public get involved?

Let's consider the growing awareness and emphasis on sustainability that have led us to question existing energy production and consumption methods. This collective rethinking has stimulated significant advances in renewable energy technologies like solar, wind, and electric vehicles. Researchers and entrepreneurs,

---

3   This definition can be found at https://www.sciencedirect.com › topics › social-sciences.

driven by a society that increasingly values sustainable practices, have been motivated to innovate and invest in renewable solutions. These experts seek new opportunities that have a substantial impact by eliminating negatives.

When you offer a solution, you want to encourage action.

In this instance, zero action is not positive. The media can inspire action on climate change by highlighting *positive* examples of individuals, communities, and organizations taking steps to reduce their carbon footprint and promote sustainability. This is the so-called "net zero effect".

On the other hand, the cultural focus on sustainability has also led to the development of new biodegradable materials, reconsiderations of agricultural practices, and even the rise of sustainable fashion. In each case, the societal value placed on sustainability has forced a re-evaluation of "the way things have always been done", leading to new ideas, technologies, and practices that might not have been considered otherwise. This is the power of the people, dictating a new order of thought. Did the media create that, or are they enthusiasts?

It's time to hit the reset button and start from zero!

In a more digitized world, cultural and societal changes will continue to provide the momentum for re-evaluating existing paradigms and creating new ones. This dynamic relationship between societal values and innovation ensures that our knowledge and technologies continually evolve, often in directions we couldn't have imagined.

Everyone wants to be included. Belonging is one of the inherent factors of human behavior, the desire to be a part of something bigger than oneself. This is why companies and corporations need to stay relevant in society. Cancel culture, fostered heavily by the younger generation, makes it imperative for businesses to reevaluate old practices to be more inclusive. They need to be aware of the impacts they have in the world, or risk lowering their client base.

Today on social media, if something is mentioned, it can eventually disappear. If some idea or product was trending today, it may no longer apply tomorrow. This could be because it has expired, or it might have been boycotted.

When boycotting, customers do not want to associate with the product and how you are selling or promoting your brand. There could be various reasons for this. It could be due to political unrest or perhaps a religious or even a personal issue. As a result, your brand then gets blocked by this audience.

Remember that all media outlets are businesses driven by the need for viewership and engagement. This reality can lead to high impact, with headlines crafted to shock rather than inform. "Negative news sells" and creates a larger audience! But such tactics can backfire, leading to public fatigue or disillusionment about the real risks associated with climate change.

With that said, media and content can and should positively address climate change by raising awareness and providing accurate and compelling information about the causes of, effects of, and potential solutions to climate change.

By shaping public opinion, media can resonate with its audiences, encouraging content creators to share and recreate ideas about it. It is like training them how to "spread the message" to circulate more content and facts about the issues in video, text, social media or podcasts, and to push these to the right audience. Thus, influencers would influence their audience by producing helpful content to raise awareness to promote a more sustainable future for all. This can influence decision-making at individual and policy levels when it trends.

Through balanced and accurate reporting, mainstream media can educate the public on the complexities of climate change, from the science behind global warming to the tangible effects already seen in various parts of the world. For instance, feature stories on shrinking glaciers, wildfires, and extreme weather events can illustrate the urgent need for action.

Unfortunately, given the 24/7 news cycle and the advent of social media, public attention can be remarkably fickle. Critical stories about the latest findings on ice melt rates or rising sea levels often get buried under breaking news or celebrity gossip. Ways have to be found to overcome this.

Documentaries can delve into causes and effects, making the issue more relatable and immediate to viewers. Spoken in Morgan Freeman's voice, it will be heard! Also, opinion pieces and editorials can advocate for policy changes and pressure lawmakers to act. If we provide a platform for experts and activists, the media can bring credibility and authority to the issue, making it difficult to ignore or dismiss. This type of journalism informs and empowers the public, giving them the knowledge and tools they need to act by changing personal habits or demanding action from their representatives.

I have always believed that responsible media reporting is crucial for battling skepticism and inactivity in an era where misinformation can spread quickly. Compelling storytelling about climate change, and whether it needs a hero to improve it, will resonate and create attention, or else who will step in? Passionate leaders with influence will play a crucial role.

False Balance

What is worse than the media not sharing the climate change case is having a "false balance". Media outlets give equal weight to climate science and climate denialism to appear impartial, thereby creating a false parity. This can dilute the message that most climate scientists agree climate change is real and primarily caused by human activities.

Could this be due to political biases? Media outlets often have political leanings, which can color their climate change coverage. For conservative outlets, this may mean downplaying the impacts or disputing the science, while liberal outlets might emphasize the dire consequences, sometimes at the expense of solutions.

The digital revolution has both eased and complicated these challenges. On one hand, social media platforms have democratized information, allowing independent journalists, scientists, and activists to convey their findings and opinions directly to the public. Interactive media, videos, and infographics can make scientific data more accessible and engaging. On the other hand, the algorithms governing these platforms often prioritize engagement over factual accuracy, facilitating the spread of misinformation. Also, the digital divide means that a large global population might lack access to this critical information.

The media has a moral obligation to evolve to create a zero-biased approach and channel the existential threat of climate change. We must see greater collaboration between journalists and scientists, the adoption of responsible reporting standards, and efforts to focus on solution-oriented stories that can go a long way in refining the narrative.

To conclude, in a world increasingly threatened by climate change, the role of media is becoming more crucial than ever. With the power to shape perceptions and drive public action, it has the potential to be a catalyst for positive change. However, achieving this potential requires overcoming significant challenges, including sensationalism, false balance, and short public attention spans. As we navigate this defining issue of our time, the media and the public are responsible for fostering an informed, balanced, and urgent lesson. Only then can we hope to make meaningful attempts to combat climate change and ensure it has a zero-problem life in the future.

■ ■ ■

Countdown to Your Zero Mindset

1. **George Monbiot's assertion**: Monbiot highlights the paradox between salience and importance in climate change discourse, emphasizing the media's role in shaping public perception.

2. **Net zero and 1.5 degrees Celsius**: These concepts, rooted in IPCC reports and the Paris Agreement, are crucial in mitigating climate change's adverse effects by balancing greenhouse gas emissions and limiting global warming.

3. **Media influence**: The media plays a significant role in shaping public opinion on climate change through accurate reporting, compelling storytelling, and highlighting positive examples and solutions.

4. **Environmental justice**: Media portrayal of climate change should prioritize environmental justice to ensure equitable burden-sharing in transitioning to sustainable practices.

5. **Societal awareness and innovation**: Growing societal awareness of sustainability drives innovation in renewable energy technologies and sustainable practices, challenging existing norms and fostering new solutions.

6. **Content creation and influence**: Content creators and influencers on social media have the power to raise awareness and influence behavior change towards sustainability.

7. **Public engagement and action**: Media coverage can inspire public engagement and action on climate change by providing credible information, showcasing real-world impacts, and advocating for policy changes.

8. **False balance and political biases**: Media outlets must avoid false balance and political biases in climate change coverage to ensure accurate representation of scientific consensus and foster informed public discourse.

9. **Digital transformation challenges**: While digital platforms democratize information, they also pose challenges such as misinformation spread and access disparities.

10. **Responsibility and collaboration**: Media has a moral obligation to evolve towards responsible reporting standards and collaborate with scientists to address climate change effectively while driving positive change.

6.5

PUZZLERS

IN THIS CHAPTER, we'll look at ideas I've encountered in my life that have puzzled me!

Let's start with the entertainment industry, which gives us mysteries, one-hit wonders, perplexing TV plots, and movies so bad they're good. Dive into these cultural riddles.

My favorite was a scene in *Mad Men* about the "99 cents" addition to a product price. What the hell is this, and how does it work?

The 99 cents pricing method is a psychological tactic where items are priced just below a complete number, such as $3.99 rather than $4.00. While it's just a one-cent difference, the psychological impact can be significant, leading consumers to perceive the price as lower than it actually is. The idea has been widely adopted in retail settings, online stores, and even service pricing, and it's rooted in several psychological principles.

Did you know that the most common way to read numbers is from left to right, so the first digit we see tends to impact our perception? Therefore, $3.99 can feel more like $3, even though it's just a cent short of $4. This rounding-down can differentiate between a sale and no sale for some consumers. But its true success is in how it aids impulse buying due to the perception of a lower price. This is especially true for things with a higher-priced item next to them. Retailers establish a price anchoring model by, for example, placing a $4.99 item next to one that is $8.99.

One of the main drawbacks is that zero is a significant accounting number in a system without fractions. The 99-cent pricing model creates a complex accounting system. It would make more sense to stick with one based on zero.

Aside from *Mad Men*, we tend to see things going viral for some odd reason, and specific content becomes wildly popular overnight. It's often hard to pinpoint why certain things go viral while others do not. I will sound a bit gross here, but what's the deal with "pimple-popping content"? (If you haven't heard of these, they're videos of people popping their pus-filled pimples.) It's trending on social media. Disgusting, right?

As we know, entertainment is often associated with celebrities, and many worship them. The fascination and glorification directed at stars can be puzzling, especially when their talents or contributions might not deserve such attention. Reality TV introduced the appeal of watching "ordinary" people in staged or exaggerated situations. It created an entire television genre, which usually results in "Fan Wars". The intensity with which people defend their favorite franchises or celebrities can be puzzling.

Here's a list of some things I don't understand. Maybe you can think about them.

- **Box office hits and misses**: Sometimes critically acclaimed films flop at the box office, while poorly-reviewed movies become hits.

- **Remakes and sequels**: Despite so many new ideas and new stories to tell, the entertainment industry often leans towards remakes.

- **High-priced art**: Paintings and other art pieces can sell for millions or even hundreds of millions of dollars, puzzling those who need help understanding the valuation of art.

- **Fast food tie-ins**: There is a growing trend of fast-food chains tying in with popular movies or shows, a marriage between entertainment and food.

- **Content overload**: In the internet age, the sheer amount of available entertainment can be overwhelming, leading to choice paralysis.

- **Music trends**: The rapid change in popular music genres and the cyclical return of past styles can be baffling.

- **Tokens in gaming**: The idea of paying small amounts of real-world money for virtual items in video games.

- **Political influences**: The role of politics in entertainment, especially in award shows or celebrity speeches, is confusing for those who seek entertainment as a form of escape.

- **Media bias**: The portrayal of events or characters can vary widely depending on the source, leading to public confusion or misinterpretation.

- **Influencer culture**: Social media influencers' rise as entertainment is a big mystery to some, especially older generations.

- **Product placement**: Sometimes, products are so seamlessly integrated that you don't realize you're being advertised to.

- **Digital vs. physical media**: Despite technological advancements, there's still a market for vinyl records, print books, and other forms of physical media.

- **Entertainment as social currency**: You must be up-to-date with certain shows, movies, or memes to be part of social conversations.

These are just a few aspects that might be puzzling or worthy of examination. The entertainment world is vast and ever-changing, and it's natural to have questions or feel perplexed.

There are many more puzzling items; I hope I triggered you to think of a few. Life often introduces us to puzzles and paradoxes that defy straightforward explanations. The domain of human experience is filled with complexities that can be confusing, unsettling, and even contradictory. Why is this?

We can feel multiple emotions simultaneously, like joy at a friend's success and envy at not achieving the same. Such complex emotional states often puzzle us as we try to navigate and make sense of them.

Despite detailed planning and preparation, life is still being determined. A venture might fail for no apparent reason; conversely, unplanned opportunities may arise and lead to success. What one culture considers ethical, another might deem immoral. These discrepancies make it difficult to establish a universally agreed-upon moral compass, leading to puzzlement when interacting across different ethical frameworks.

Do We Like to be Victims?

Many people contemplate why bad things happen to good people or why suffering exists. Philosophers, theologians, and thinkers have wrestled with this existential question for centuries without arriving at a universally accepted answer. Human relationships are fraught with misunderstandings, unspoken feelings, and subtle dynamics that are often hard to define. Why some relationships thrive while others fail can be puzzling, even in hindsight.

I call it the Complexity of Simple Things, where something as simple as happiness can be puzzling. What makes one person happy might not necessarily work for another, and the search for happiness often leads to more questions than answers.

Overall, life is a mix of chaos and order. While humans strive for predictability and control, unforeseen events and the unpredictable nature of other people add clutter to our lives, making the world an intricate puzzle. The perplexity of life often arises from its intrinsic complexity, the limitations of human understanding, and the complicated interplay between countless variables. While some find this uncertainty discomforting, others see it as what makes life intriguing, providing opportunities for growth, wisdom, and deepening human experience. What is puzzling to one may not be to another. This may lead to people having strong opinions on others or strong feelings towards others based on their knowledge. The concept of having haters and handling criticism will be discussed in the next chapter.

■ ■ ■

Countdown to Your Zero Mindset

1. The "99 cents" pricing strategy exploits psychological principles, making prices appear lower than they are.

2. The fascination with celebrities and reality TV highlights the puzzling nature of entertainment preferences.

3. Box office hits and misses, remakes, and sequels often defy expectations, confusing audiences.

4. The valuation of high-priced art and the integration of fast-food tie-ins with entertainment raise questions about value and consumer behavior.

5. Content overload in the internet age and rapidly changing music trends can overwhelm and confuse consumers.

6. Tokens in gaming, political influences in entertainment, and media bias add layers of complexity to the industry.

7. Influencer culture, product placement, and the coexistence of digital and physical media challenge traditional entertainment norms.

8. Entertainment as social currency and the complexity of human relationships underscore the multifaceted nature of the industry.

9. Life's existential puzzles, ethical discrepancies, and the complexity of simple things add layers of intrigue and confusion to human experience.

7

NO OFFENSE

SAYING "NO OFFENSE" before offending: Does the preface make the subsequent comment less offensive?

Does it make zero sense?

I read once that haters are secret admirers. And they ARE! You might disagree with me, but trust me, believing they are secret admirers makes your life easier and theirs harder. It helps it all make sense!

Don't you just love that people who are consistently negative or critical towards someone might be driven by hidden admiration or jealousy? Honestly, the idea is that "haters" concentrate their energy on you because they see something in you they can't be.

That's terrific! It is your qualities, success, or even the potential in you that they admire, desire, feel threatened by. Or maybe they just hate themselves. The notion that "haters are secret admirers" suggests a psychological dynamic where individuals express negativity or criticism as a defense mechanism to conceal underlying feelings of admiration or positive emotions.

Under the scope of psychoanalytic theory, a subset of psychology pioneered by Sigmund Freud, such defense mechanisms can occur unconsciously and are a part of everyday life. This perspective highlights the complexity of human behavior. One defense mechanism is projection, where individuals attribute feelings about themselves onto the target of their criticism. Additionally, expressions of hate may stem from jealousy or envy, fear of rejection, or a desire for attention, presenting a multifaceted interplay of emotions and motivations.

However, it's crucial to approach this concept with caution, as human behavior is diverse and influenced by various factors. Not all instances of hate can be linked to secret admiration. This would oversimplify the intricate nature of individual emotions and relationships. People's motivations for expressing negativity can be driven by personal insecurities, past experiences, or fundamental differences in values and perspectives. Acknowledging the complexity of human emotions and avoiding broad generalizations is essential for a nuanced understanding of individual behavior.

Feedback is a Gift

It's also vital to understand that not all criticism arises from admiration or envy. Constructive criticism can be helpful in growth and improvement. My friend Dr. Fouad M. Alame said to me once, "Feedback is a gift." Powerful, right? It takes maturity to appreciate feedback. Of course, it's crucial to differentiate between helpful feedback and destructive feedback or unnecessary negativity. Again, someone might give out such negativity due to their own personal issues or insecurities.

Knowing how and when to handle criticism constructively, including knowing when it's practical for self-improvement, is valuable. Destructive criticism should be ignored. Here is an example of criticism exchanged between rival media agencies, showing that handling criticism well can emphasize your power. Two agencies stood out like peacocks at a pigeon party in the advertising world: "Company A" and "Company B". Their rivalry was legendary, but not in the way you might think. Rather than mortal enemies locked in cutthroat competition, they operated more like sarcastic roommates perpetually pranking each other.

Industry insiders knew them as "zero lovers", two agencies that always seemed to be throwing oddly affectionate jabs at each other's campaigns. "Hey, Dany," said Patrick, the Creative Director at one agency, bumping into Dany, the Executive Producer, at an awards ceremony. "I saw your new ad campaign. Loved how the camera focused on the bubbles for dramatic effect. Almost forgot I was watching soap and not a brand in the ad!"

Dany laughed. "No offense, Patrick, but given your agency's recent commercial featuring a talking product, I thought you'd appreciate our shift towards high art."

"None taken! Our talking product, Salma, is a queen and you know it."

The two agencies were masters at crafting unforgettable advertisements, and they always seemed to release their most groundbreaking work within weeks of each other. When Company A created a viral ad featuring a dancing giraffe to promote an energy drink, Company B countered with a visually stunning ad featuring a skydiving team of grandmothers.

"Your skydiving grandmas were chaotic. We had a good laugh at the office."

"Thanks! Your Giraffe had us all attempting to dance at our last team meeting. Our CFO pulled a muscle."

The playful banter extended to social media. Company A messaged: "No offense to our friends, but our giraffe can out-dance any skydiving grandma. #DancingGiraffeVsSkydivingGrandma," to which Company B replied: "Challenge accepted, @Agency. Our grandmas have some moves you've never seen! #BringItOnToUs."

As unconventional as it seemed, this unique "zero lovers" rivalry drove both agencies to be more creative, edgy, and daring. Clients were intrigued by the agencies' playful opposition and even started to see it as a quirky form of quality assurance: If you could survive and thrive in the world of zero lovers, you were clearly doing something right.

Ultimately, both agencies understood a crucial point many others in their hypercompetitive industry missed. Sometimes, the best way to rise is not by tearing each other down but by playfully pushing each other to improve. And if you could have some fun and share a few laughs along the way, that was the icing on the cake.

This is a fictional depiction of the advertising world, but "No Offense (Zero Lovers)" illustrates how competition doesn't have to be mean-spirited or destructive. Instead, it can be a source of inspiration and harmony, pushing everyone to reach new heights of creativity and effectiveness.

Their business relationship defied conventional wisdom. They recognized that their rivalry could coexist with respect and perhaps even a sort of affection for each other's ingenuity and business understanding.

So, they remained zero lovers, competitors who shared a marketplace but never offended each other to the point of hostility. They realized that sometimes the most potent competition comes not from undermining your rivals but pushing yourself to improve, spurred on by their presence. And so, Company A and Company B continued to grow, not despite each other, but perhaps *because* of each other in a strange way. It was the gracefulness in which they would handle criticism to push their company forward rather than hold them back. Sometimes taking zero offense is the best choice, because it instills self-reflection and serves as a driving factor to push past uncertain moments.

■ ■ ■

Countdown to Your Zero Mindset

1. Prefacing offensive remarks with "no offense" does not make them less offensive.

2. The concept that "haters are secret admirers" suggests a psychological dynamic where criticism stems from underlying positive feelings or envy.

3. Human behavior, influenced by defense mechanisms like projection and jealousy, can contribute to expressions of hate or negativity.

4. Constructive criticism can be valuable for growth, but distinguishing between helpful feedback and destructive negativity is essential.

5. A fictional rivalry between advertising agencies exemplifies playful banter and competition without hostility, fostering creativity and improvement.

6. In manufacturing, two companies maintain a playful rivalry, mimicking each other's marketing gimmicks without hostility.

7. Both examples illustrate how competition can coexist with respect and even affection, leading to mutual growth and improvement.

8. The idea of taking zero offense allows for self-reflection and can serve as a driving force for personal and professional development.

9. Handling criticism gracefully can lead to positive outcomes, fostering innovation and pushing past obstacles.

10. Ultimately, the ability to navigate criticism constructively contributes to individual and organizational success in competitive environments.

8

PINEAPPLE ON PIZZA (THINGS THAT DON'T MAKE SENSE)

THE PINEAPPLE ON pizza debate creates a lot of "side-eyes". Is it a culinary marvel or a taste caricature? Below, you can pick and choose what makes zero sense. We are in the nonsense category here, and the following comes from some of my real-life situations.

Did you ever question why pizza comes in a round serving, though it comes in a square box, and you cut it in triangular slices? I mean who invented pizza, the Italians or a mathematician?

How many times do we sit in meetings and leave with outcomes that are mostly forgotten? Is this poor management skills, or do we just want these meetings to be over so we can get on with our work the way we like to do it? When I was a kid at school, the only thing that mattered was the clock hitting the end of the hour so the bell would ring and we could have recess. Is this "school effect" contributing to endless meetings with no actionable outcomes?

On many occasions, I have been invited to company outings or so-called team building. This rarely results in a better workplace environment. As above, we just want it to be over! It just doesn't make sense to me, as though it's mandatory to have fun on these occasions (which has never been the case, by the way). And since we're talking about office matters, what about office politics? I mean, come on; this is the most destructive behavior in a work environment. Gossip and backstabbing have become the most recognizable issues in the workplace today; staff waste time on nonsense and non-productive behavior that leads to poor teamwork and negative results.

What About Hot Desking?

COVID has accelerated the reduction of costs due to people working from home. Your home office space became your safe space, leading to a lonely environment and lack of belonging. Yes it was a good way to reduce costs, but that feeling when you get to your desk in the office and see your personal belongings, like pictures, notes and scribbles, means something to you. These days, with hot desking, you need to clear your desk as if you are renting a space in a coffee shop. This makes you feel like a stranger, coming to the office and finding a different seat every time. Not cool!

People might hate me for this, but having unlimited vacation policies that serve only the employee is not productive. People need to be accountable for their work and commit to results and timetables. Freedom will result in individual happiness, but too much also contributes to laziness. We all get lazy sometimes, but we need a form of discipline when we are employed. We aren't getting a salary to act on our own merit; we need to deliver results to management and, more importantly, convey commitment within an organization and in front of our colleagues to show solidarity.

What I hate the most is the Monday sick leaves. This is unacceptable; the weekend is made to decompress and gather yourself for another week of work. Instead, we use the weekend to celebrate and ignore our duties ahead. It is no wonder that we've seen many companies shut down due to lack of performance as they've become too soft. I am not saying that mental wellness isn't important, but it is being taken for granted by employees.

In many cases, management is also at fault when they have complex organization charts. People need structure and proper authority. It's imperative that we describe roles in an organization in a simple and structured way, so our staff can understand where to go when they have questions in need of answers (whether it's their boss or HR or the CEO, etc.), or when they are in a situation where they need to feel protected.

Disorganized Sense

How many times you have heard the phrase "back-to-back meetings"? Oh, how this annoys me. I mean, how poorly must you be organized to make no time between meetings for something better? The audacity that comes with this idea is just stupid and sounds like a joke! I just hate it.

I am sure you have seen someone getting promoted based on their current performance instead of their ability to perform their new task. This is called "The Peter Principle" and it has been recognized and ridiculed in some companies. The concept was explained in the 1969 book *The Peter Principle* by Laurence Peter and Raymond Hull. Hull wrote the text, based on Peter's research. Peter and Hull intended the book to be satire, but it became popular as it was seen to make a serious point about the shortcomings of how people are promoted within hierarchical organizations. The Peter Principle has since been the subject of much commentary and research.

I used to be an advocate for dress codes. Maybe I still am somehow, but suits and ties don't necessarily enhance productivity.

I mean, if you are in the office and have no meetings, loosen up a bit and be comfortable. DO NOT come in shorts or sandals, but be flexible in your outfit.

On another note, I remember twenty-five years ago when I started my career, I was working in a great company, but they had this weird open office plan where everyone was sitting together. They called it a Japanese setting. Personally, I never understood why it was important, but it sure as hell made me feel watched every second of every day. It was very discouraging, conveying a lack of trust as well as being a bit distracting. However, in hindsight, it made me work more (or at least pretend I was working).

Emails, oh how I hate emails. Everyone wants to send you an email, internal or external. We spend so much time organizing and going through emails, and what really gets on my nerves is emails from people sitting next to you addressing you directly with everyone cc'd. I mean come on, what are they trying to prove? The worst is when a colleague emails you and cc's your boss; this is the modern way of threating someone. Unacceptable. Will we ever work in an environment with a zero email policy? Can we get on with our work and what really matters? Don't you also question why companies also lay off people when the year ends with positive results? What's the deal with that? Are they so unsure about next year that they feel a lack of confidence about what they will deliver? Is this a lack of vision? Is it shareholder concern over results and employee wellbeing? What about the year after that? Does no one want to worry that far forward? Or is it just bonus-related?

Of Zero Substance

Do you know the term "golden parachutes" for failed executives? It's a big payout for top executives who don't perform, something that happens to them in the long term when they see only the short-term picture! And still they get rewarded. Buzzwords are mostly made up to make others sound smarter, and make you feel stupid! There is an overload of unnecessary jargon that confuses us more than clarifying anything.

I work in ad tech. We use the abbreviation CPM a lot, which means cost per mille. Mille is a French word that means thousand, but because we work in an English environment, and no one actually knows what the M stands for, we started using CPT (cost per thousand). While 'mille' in French means one thousand, one mile in English means a value of approximately 1600 metres, not one thousand. Urghhh!

Okay, I am on a roll here. The phrase "the customer is always right" just gets to me: Most of the time, they are not! Again, I work in marketing and advertising, and clients come to us to help them solve a problem or deliver something new. Our role here is to disrupt or do something better or different. When someone is paying you to do something, they should expect you to be better than they are rather than spoon-feeding you the answers they want. Why come to you in the first place if they have all the answers?

Maybe in retail the idea serves a purpose, since you just want to sell, but how can you deliver the right attitude if the customer just wants what they want? On the flip side, and to be fair, salespeople also sometimes oversell, which results in a bad experience overall.

I am sure you have had the experience of calling a hotline and you get customer service sitting somewhere in a different time zone. The conversation just doesn't click. You feel you are talking to a human robot that answers you from a dashboard of "frequently asked questions". It is so stupid and irritating. I mean, outsourcing customer service is just bad for business and loyalty. Horrible idea! I could rant about many bad company decisions. Maybe I should write a book about it. For instance: paying for a software license that no one uses, just adding costs to keep someone job-busy and worth their salary. Or a company buying a ping-pong table to increase job happiness or security. All it does is create an illusion of perks in the office.

I remember when I was applying for colleges, back in the day when we applied via mail. When I didn't get accepted, I wasn't refunded for my job application. I mean, facing the shame of not getting through and not getting a refund was just mind-blowing.

I felt like an idiot. Please, colleges, refund people when you don't accept them; it's the right thing to do.

What about celebrity-endorsed products? Do celebrities use all the products they endorse? Who follows up on this? I have seen many so-called influencers promote a car that they are not driving or a clothing brand they can't afford and don't like; that's just silly.

Talking about silly things, what about coffee table books? They are often more for show than actual reading. Are they still a thing?

In daily life, I have witnessed many uncomfortable situations. Urinals, for example. They are too wide open, zero privacy!

I have also witnessed this first hand: Someone was putting milk in before the cereal. How can you do such a thing? It is always cereal before milk; please, folks.

Talking about food, I have to mention airline food, just horrible and messy. I still don't understand why people devour this food. Buy your own sandwich and just eat it on the plane, or try to sleep; you don't need to eat on a short flight.

Also, what is it with people wearing sunglasses indoors? Is this fashion over function? If you want to hide your eyes, just put on a mask and spare us from this fashion disaster.

I will conclude now with some funny things I have witnessed, and I am sure we have all been in similar situations before. The elevator! In elevators we have to listen to garbage music. There is no DJ in an elevator, so let's just kill this idea, maybe small talk is a nicer approach? And what about people entering the elevator before others exit? How annoying is that? Especially when it opens on the ground level!

Let's Get Serious Again

Life is inherently complex, full of variables that can change at any moment. This complexity can make it difficult to predict outcomes or understand why things happen the way they do. Sometimes events occur with no reason or pattern, adding to the chaos and the feeling that life doesn't make sense. The feeling that things make "no sense" in life and business is common, causing confusion, frustration, or uncertainty. However, there may be multiple factors at play that contribute to this perception.

Our perspective is naturally limited by our own experiences, biases, and available information, which can restrict our ability to fully grasp situations. Our emotional state can cloud our judgment and make it difficult to see the logic or reason in cases. Philosophical and existential questions about the meaning of life, why we're here, and our purpose can also contribute to a sense that things don't make sense.

In business, we understand that markets are influenced by an almost infinite number of factors, economic indicators, political events, and consumer sentiment, to name just a few, and all of these can cause a number of unpredictable outcomes. Business involves dealing with people, and people can be unpredictable. Decision-making can be influenced by emotional, irrational, or unpredictable factors. Look at some governments; they can change or introduce new rules, making the business environment unstable or confusing. The actions of competitors can sometimes seem irrational or unpredictable, affecting your business in ways that don't make sense.

Today, rapid technological advancements can render existing business models obsolete, making it seem like the rules are constantly changing.

How to cope, then? Well, the more you learn about the variables affecting a situation, the more sense you can make of it.

We need to accept uncertainty: Knowing or controlling everything is impossible. Sometimes, you have to admit that things may not always make sense. Sometimes, talking to others can offer new perspectives that help you make sense of things. Being flexible and willing to adapt can help you navigate times when things make little sense.

Be mindful and reflect: Taking time to reflect can offer insights into why things are the way they are. It can be frustrating when life or business seems illogical or confusing, but it's often just a matter of perspective. As you gain more experience and understanding, things may start to make more sense, or at least become easier to navigate.

But please, everyone: No pineapple on pizza anymore!

■ ■ ■

Countdown to Your Zero Mindset

1. Various real-life situations question the logic behind common practices and phenomena.

2. We look at office dynamics, meeting inefficiencies, and management practices, highlighting areas of frustration and confusion.

3. Critiques are offered on topics such as hot desking, unlimited vacation policies, and Monday sick leaves, questioning their effectiveness.

4. The concept of the Peter Principle is introduced, discussing how individuals may be promoted based on current performance rather than suitability for new roles.

5. Emphasizing the need for acceptance of uncertainty, reflection, and adaptation to navigate through times when things may not make sense.

9

THE ART OF NOTHING

HAVE YOU EVER tried to do nothing? Or, as the Dutch call it, "niksen".

It's time to relax and disconnect from your busy lives, like taking a break from your phone, work, and being productive. This chapter will look at why it is important to balance your work life with rest, and all the benefits that come with doing absolutely ZILCH.

LIVE in the present moment!

While it may seem difficult in our fast-paced society, doing nothing can benefit your mental and physical health. It could reduce stress, improve focus and creativity, and increase feelings of enjoyment and wellbeing. Here are some "nothing" ideas I enjoy:

1. Sitting outside and enjoying nature without any distractions.

2. Taking my car and driving somewhere without worrying about where.

3. Listening to something soothing without any other distractions.

4. Sitting in silence.

5. Playing backgammon.

6. Looking at art.

Some call it "The art of doing nothing." I'll tell you: It takes work!

So How Do You Do It?

Just allow yourself to be in the moment without any specific expectations. So, take time to slow down, disconnect from technology, and enjoy the art of doing nothing, the art of zero; you will thank yourself. Remember, you're doing nothing for no reason, so don't return to doing something! As Jerry Seinfeld said,

"Watch out, though, doing nothing might lead to doing something, which might interrupt you from doing nothing!"

If you were to really think about it, when was the last time you did nothing?

The idea that doing nothing can have value may seem counterintuitive in cultures that prize constant activity and productivity. However, taking time to do nothing can offer a range of benefits, both for individual wellbeing and for improving productivity in work and other activities. It benefits your mental health. This is because constant activity and "busyness" can contribute to stress, while taking breaks can help reduce this stress. Periods of doing nothing can help clear your mind and lead to better decision-making, and time spent in inactive reflection can enhance self-understanding, helping you become more attuned to your own needs and aspirations.

A *Time* magazine article written in February of 2023 explored the concept of doing nothing and its potential productivity benefits. The author, Gloria Mark, who has a PhD in psychology and is a professor at the University of California, explores the societal pressure for constant productivity and the negative impact it can have on mental health and wellbeing. Drawing on insights from experts, the article discusses the importance of embracing moments of idleness and the value of unstructured time for creativity, problem-solving, and overall cognitive function. It challenges the prevailing notion that constant busyness equates to success and emphasizes the significance of downtime in fostering personal growth and maintaining a balanced, healthy life. The piece encouraged readers to reconsider their attitudes toward idleness and highlighted the positive outcomes of allowing the mind to rest and recharge. Doing zero boosts creativity when you step away from a problem or task and can allow your mind to work on it unconsciously, often leading to unexpected and creative solutions. Rest can improve your focus when you return to work, making your efforts more effective. A clear mind can more easily tackle problems and develop innovative solutions.

Your body needs time to rest and repair itself. Doing nothing gives your body this much-needed time. It improves health, as reduced stress and better mental health are strongly correlated with physical health benefits, like a more robust immune system and lower risk of chronic disease. As Joseph Brodsky, a Russian-American poet and essayist, said, "Doing nothing offers our brains the ability to recover."

I remember reading another article that underscored the importance of allocating time for idleness as a beneficial practice for emotional wellbeing. It challenged the prevailing cultural norm of constant productivity and busyness, arguing that embracing moments of doing nothing can lead to reduced stress and heightened emotional resilience. The piece featured insights from Dr. Kelly Donahue, a clinical psychologist, who emphasized the therapeutic value of downtime. Dr. Donahue noted, "In our culture, there's so much focus on productivity and achievement, we often forget that our bodies and minds need time to rest and recharge. By giving yourself permission to do nothing, you're saying that you matter, too."

The article explored how "doing nothing" can enhance creativity and problem-solving abilities. Dr. Donahue reinforces this perspective, stating, "Doing nothing allows your mind to wander, and that's often where you can find the most creative solutions to problems." The article concluded by encouraging readers to prioritize moments of idleness in their lives, recognizing the potential benefits for mental health and overall wellbeing.

Doing Nothing Socially

Doing nothing can be shared with loved ones, strengthening your relationships. It enhances emotional space to process feelings and events, helping you regulate emotions more effectively. And it allows for deep thought and existential reflection, fostering a sense of peace or spiritual wellbeing. "Be Present", they say in *Kung Fu Panda*. The present is a gift; it encourages mindfulness instead of constantly thinking about the next item on your to-do list.

Constant work and activity can lead to burnout. Doing nothing is a way to prevent this. Living in the moment can help you appreciate what you have right now instead of constantly seeking more or worrying about what you don't have. It also deepens self-awareness; being in the NOW can lead to a deeper understanding of yourself and your own needs, desires, and feelings.

It's important to note that while living in the present has many benefits, planning for the future and learning from the past are also crucial. The idea is not to disregard the past or future entirely, but to not let them become detached from your current experience. Blending the past, present, and future in a balanced way is vital to a well-rounded life.

Be sustainable in your productivity; in the long run, balancing work with rest can lead to more sustainable productivity levels than the peaks and troughs associated with a constant push for output. While "doing nothing" might seem like a waste of time on the surface, its benefits are multifaceted and significant. It provides a holistic approach to wellbeing and effectiveness in life's various endeavors. This may be hard to accept. I will expand on the notion of acceptance in the next chapter which, luckily for you, is the last one.

■ ■ ■

Countdown to Your Zero Mindset

1. The concept of "Niksen" or doing nothing is explored as a way to relax and disconnect from busy lives.

2. Benefits of doing nothing include reduced stress, improved focus and creativity, and increased feelings of enjoyment and wellbeing.

3. Examples of "nothing" activities include sitting outside, driving without a destination, listening to soothing sounds, and sitting in silence.

4. Embracing moments of idleness can lead to better decision-making, enhanced self-understanding, and increased creativity.

5. Time spent doing nothing allows the mind to rest and recharge, improving mental health and reducing stress.

6. Doing nothing socially can strengthen relationships, enhance emotional regulation, and foster peace or spiritual wellbeing.

7. Prioritizing moments of idleness in life is encouraged for mental health and overall wellbeing.

8. Living in the present moment encourages mindfulness and appreciation of what one has.

9. Balancing work with rest is essential for sustainable productivity and overall wellbeing.

10. While doing nothing may seem unproductive, its benefits contribute to a holistic approach to wellbeing and effectiveness in life.

10

ACCEPTANCE

ACCEPTING ONE'S FAULTS and returning to a "zero base" is a courageous step that often signifies a turning point in personal and professional development. This concept aligns with "radical self-awareness", wherein individuals confront their shortcomings, weaknesses, and even failures, not as self-criticism but as a foundation to build a more authentic and competent self.

Confronting your own faults can be emotionally draining but also incredibly liberating. The process involves setting aside ego, societal expectations, and sometimes even the opinions of people who matter to you. Accepting that you have flaws and made mistakes can lead to psychological freedom. It lifts the weight of pretending to be perfect or having all the answers. This level of self-awareness often serves as a catalyst for emotional growth and resilience. Recognizing and accepting our imperfections can also make us more empathetic toward others, strengthening our relationships and improving our social skills.

Starting from a "zero base" is like hitting the reset button on a computer; it allows the system to operate more efficiently by eliminating errors and clearing out unnecessary clutter. When you return to zero in life or your career, you can reassess your goals, strategies, and the steps needed to achieve them. From a growth standpoint, this is invaluable. It presents an opportunity to pivot and realign with objectives that fit your redefined sense of self more.

This could mean changing career paths, improving previously neglected skills, or even re-evaluating personal relationships to see if they align with your newfound perspective.

To many of us, acceptance is not as easy as it might seem; again, we are creatures of habit, and sometimes, accepting change lies thicker on us than the reality of its necessities. The difficulty in accepting things, whether circumstances, outcomes, or traits about ourselves or others, often stems from a complex interplay of psychological factors, cultural norms, and individual experiences. Accepting a new reality usually means reconciling it with our existing beliefs, which can create cognitive dissonance and psychological stress.

Coined by psychologist Leon Festinger in 1957, the term "cognitive dissonance" describes the psychological stress or discomfort experienced by an individual who holds two or more contradictory beliefs, values, or perceptions at the same time. For example, someone who values health but smokes cigarettes might experience cognitive dissonance. To clear the dissonance, the individual may change a belief or action, like quitting smoking or downplaying health risks.

The change affects our ego and self-identity. Our self-concept can be threatened when we have to accept something that does not align with how we see ourselves or want to be seen by others. When ego and self-identity intersect, it can make acceptance difficult. According to Sigmund Freud, both ego and self-identity are complex psychological constructs that help us make sense of ourselves and the world around us. They influence our ability or willingness to accept new realities, as the ego is part of the threefold model of the mind in psychoanalytic theory, which also includes the id and the superego. It intervenes between our elementary desires and our moral or social constraints. Our ego is fundamentally concerned with self-preservation and often aims to protect us from internal or external discomfort. A shield we possess when faced with information or a reality that contradicts our self-image, the ego may deploy defense mechanisms like denial, repression, or rationalization to avoid accepting that new information. These mechanisms can misinterpret our perception of reality to maintain balance, making acceptance demanding.

Self-identity is our internal self-concept, our individualism, a collection of beliefs, attributes, and roles that defines us. Usually, we are shaped by both internal factors (like personal experiences and features) and external factors (such as cultural norms and social expectations). Cognitive dissonance occurs when we encounter a situation that requires us to accept something with our self-identity. This anticipation makes it hard to integrate the new reality into our existing self-concept, leading to emotional discomfort, confusion, or even a sense of betrayal to oneself.

When ego and self-identity cross, our ego aims to protect this self-identity. Any threat to one often provokes an involuntary response from the other. For example, if someone is ethical but faces a situation where they have acted unethically, their ego and self-identity are threatened. The ego might activate defense mechanisms like denial ("I didn't do anything wrong") or rationalization ("It's not that big a deal; everyone does it") to avoid accepting this hard truth.

Fear of the Unknown

We are constantly threatened by fear of the unknown. Accepting change is a form of uncertainty; it's like surrendering control, which may be one reason most people would rather avoid change. Change can lead to a negative balance, a minus. It is a return to neutral that we want, to zero equilibrium to enable us to be balanced.

It can be hard for individuals to accept things that society deems damaging. Culture is entrenched in tradition; many faiths and beliefs dictate collective acceptance and denial, which may seem like an injustice. We are taught about philosophers from ancient history being accused of treason due to their groundbreaking thoughts and theories toward life, science, and religion. Collective denial occurs when entire communities or societies struggle with acceptance, such as recognizing historical injustices.

For decades, tobacco companies engaged in a campaign of denial and misinformation, actively concealing and disputing scientific evidence linking smoking to serious health risks such as lung cancer, heart disease, and respiratory ailments. It was not until the mid-20th Century, when the scientific evidence became overwhelming and public awareness grew, that governments began implementing regulations and public health initiatives to curb smoking rates and protect public health. In modern times, we see another form of stigma regarding accepting mental health issues.

Accepting change is not easy, but it is necessary in life. It requires us to embody certain personality traits. Being open to new ideas and cultures, adapting to change, and overcoming fear are essential. We are not bulletproof; not everyone is emotionally resilient. Some people may not yet have developed the emotional tools needed for acceptance, making any form of it a significant personal struggle.

One thing I would like to leave you with is the importance to forgive and/or forget. Equally important is the ability to move forward in your life. Try not to hold onto baggage from the past as it will always haunt you. Whether you choose to forgive or forget or even both, it is necessary for your mindfulness and wellbeing.

In summary, yielding to a zero base by acknowledging one's faults is not an admission of defeat but rather an empowering act of self-realization. It gives you the psychological freedom to be more authentically yourself and offers a clean slate from which you can chart a more purposeful and fulfilling course.

Try to use the everyday expression "It makes zero sense" while dealing with change and overcoming contradictions and ambiguities. The phrase is not about accepting zero in its negative sense, but the presence of balance and, in a way, a healthy confusion of existence.

This book is a call to rethink your life, your actions, and your inactions. The idea of zero and the elimination of negatives encourages individuals to take a proactive and intentional approach to their lives. By identifying and removing negative influences, habits, and distractions, you can create a more focused, productive, and fulfilling life that aligns with your values and goals. It's a call to rethink and reshape one's life for the better.

Believe me, this is the hardest thing you will do in your life. Whether it's in your business or personal life, embracing a zero mindset will allow you to step back and *re*think things through.

The goal is to start, and zero is always the starting point on your grid. I will share with you one last thing, and then you are off the hook. Life has to start somewhere, and it always starts from nothingness. I am on a journey of self-discovery, and will always be on it. It's normal never to reach the end, just as it is normal not to reach zero. Infinity and zero are quite similar, as both are aspirations towards ultimate possibilities; one is the possibility of growing and becoming bigger and the latter is about doing this right from the start.

If you are starting over, then you must have learned from your errors. That's what we do, right? So, if you are in a place to redo things or wish to be more perfect, I encourage you to do things with a zero mindset. Begin properly and you shall travel better and with more comfort. You might not reach the greater destination, but you shall reach the destination in a great way! Choose wisely when deciding how you do things in your life and do not be tempted to hide faults and expect them not to be noticed. Aim for perfection, as you are responsible for your performance.

Overall, your beginning is always a motivation and a call to take action. You should force yourself to approach your life with intention and a commitment to continuous improvement. It encourages you to embrace the idea of starting over and striving for excellence, ultimately leading to a more fulfilling and purpose-driven life.

I welcome you to "begin again", but now with a zero mindset! If this makes zero sense to you, then we are on the same page.

■ ■ ■

Countdown to Your Zero Mindset

1. Accepting faults and returning to a "zero base" signifies a courageous step in personal and professional development.

2. "Radical self-awareness" involves confronting shortcomings and failures as a foundation for growth, not self-criticism.

3. Acceptance of flaws can lead to psychological freedom and emotional growth by lifting the weight of perfectionism.

4. Returning to a "zero base" allows for reassessment of goals, strategies, and personal relationships, leading to realignment with one's sense of self.

5. Cognitive dissonance occurs when conflicting beliefs or perceptions create psychological stress, making acceptance challenging.

6. Ego and self-identity play significant roles in acceptance, as they influence how individuals perceive new realities that contradict their self-image.

7. Fear of the unknown can hinder acceptance, as it involves surrendering control and uncertainty about the outcome.

8. Cultural norms and societal expectations can make it difficult for individuals and communities to accept change or recognize injustices.

9. Mental wellness stigma can also impede acceptance, but acknowledging faults and embracing change is necessary for personal growth.

10. Embracing a "zero mindset" involves starting anew with intention and commitment to continuous improvement, leading to a more fulfilling and purpose-driven life.

AUTHOR BIO

Patrick brings together a potent trio of media, data, and technology to revolutionize the ways businesses and publications interact and create both for and with their audiences. An accomplished CEO and entrepreneur, he is a visionary leader whose experience in marketing, commercial finance, and digital operations lends him a unique perspective on digital transformation and revenue generation.

Patrick's 27-year career in media and advertising has seen him at the helm of various renowned multinational brands, leading their growth and digital strategy.

The driving force bringing some of global media's most prominent offerings to the MENA region, Patrick launched MTV Networks channels into the region as the General Manager of Viacom.

His keen eye for promising opportunities also led him to play an instrumental role in bringing the Virgin Radio brand to the UAE.

Later, as the MENA Regional Head at Zee Entertainment Enterprises, he introduced and managed Zee Arabic business in the region and relaunched the way Arabs perceive Bollywood.

These media launches came at a crucial period of growth for the industry in the region, and Patrick emerged as a pioneering leader in establishing viable business strategies in entertainment and media.

From spearheading broadcast network launches, Patrick moved on to become the Chief Commercial Officer at Sky News Arabia, where he headed revenue business for the news organization's TV, radio, online, and mobile platforms.

In this role, Patrick successfully introduced a variety of brands and programs under Sky News Arabia. In addition, by creating opportunities for monetization, he integrated new revenue streams within the network, strategically building an innovative commercial system that could support the business's strategic growth.

At this point, Patrick decided to embark on a new adventure, leaving full-time employment to venture into entrepreneurship. He is currently the Founder and Group CEO of many mar-tech companies and the founder of Ink Worldwide.

His portfolio of companies caters to diverse region-relevant audiences. They provide e-commerce and media organizations with a data-driven platform that uses intelligent tech to fast-track their growth.

With a master's degree in Marketing, Media and Communication from Paris Sorbonne University and a bachelor's degree in Business and Management, Patrick is well-placed to offer intelligent insights on the intersection of media, technology, creativity, and revenue. He expresses fresh perspectives and unconventional opinions with his signature sense of humor, making for engaging discussions that endear him to hosts and audiences alike.

Patrick's career became apparent to him after he first watched satellite television. For the first time, he was fascinated by international and regional commercials, awards shows, and sporting events.

Sounds clichéd, right? But in the 90s, the commercials were even more powerful than the content, being local, relatable, and relevant to the viewer. Patrick started questioning the source of advertisements and campaigns. He wanted to know the origin of the scripts and how they became real.

This passion for advertising sparked a 27-year media and digital transformation career across multinational companies in the GCC and Middle East, which led him to where he is today—the head of a group of media, e-commerce, and tech-based companies that provide end-to-end solutions to their partners and advertisers in Middle East and international markets.

Patrick helps publishers grow their reach and monetize their traffic, and assists e-commerce brands in acquiring new customer bases with the help of tech-driven solutions. This allows clients to understand their customers' behavior and customize their experience.

Sound interesting? Let's chat.

EXTRAS

To download your free digital copy of this book, head to www.itmakeszerosense.com, or order it directly form the website.

Patrick Samaha is also available on LinkedIn (https://www.linkedin.com/in/patrick-samaha), or you can connect with him through the website.

Patrick is an accomplished entrepreneur, author, and public speaker who is available for corporate or other events, where he can speak on "the zero mindset" and much more. If you are entering the media world or the Gulf region and you wish to use his consulting services, please do not hesitate to engage.

Individuals, entrepreneurs, or start-ups can also benefit from Patrick's consultancy. Reach out at patrick@itmakeszerosense.com to get started.

Notes